Immanuel

Reflections
on the Life
of Christ

Immanuel

Reflections
on the Life
of Christ

MICHAEL CARD

Thomas Nelson Publishers
Nashville

❖ *A Janet Thoma Book* ❖

Library of Congress Cataloging-in-Publication Data

Card, Michael, 1957–
    Immanuel : reflections on the life of Christ / Michael Card.
      p.   cm.
    ISBN 0-8407-7496-6
    1. Jesus Christ—Biography—Devotional literature. 2. Jesus
Christ—Poetry. I. Title.
BT306.5.C37 1990
232.9′01—dc20
  [B]

90-37978
CIP

To my wife, Susan,
who is as committed
to my life of reflection
as she is to her own

CONTENTS

THE INCARNATION

THE MINISTRY

THE PASSION

In Him was life, and the life was the light of men.

Last year I experienced a crisis with words which was precipitated by an encounter with Silence. What came home to me very powerfully was that silence really does say more than words. God speaks to us in the silence of the heart. Spoken or sung, words usually interfere with God's will as much as they help in seeing it done.

For someone like me, a "vendor of words," this was a discouraging experience. When a new record was released that year it was disheartening to look at the blank bands between the songs on the L.P. and wonder if perhaps they might contain more meaning than the grooves that contained the music and lyrics I had labored over for so many months!

Something Soren Kierkegaard had said finally dawned on me: "Be silent, for that is the Absolute."

Thankfully, the Lord didn't leave me desolate in this crisis. He used the experience to give me a whole new appreciation both for words as well as His Word. I was compelled to do my best to choose words with more care rather than to give up on them altogether.

In contrast to the sullen word of Ecclesiastes 12:12, "of making many books there is no end," the words of John 21:25 (NKJV) came to life: "And there are also many other things that Jesus did, which if they were written one by one, I suppose that even the world itself could not contain the books that would be written."

It was not until I despaired of using words that, oddly enough, I felt ready to try to write a book full of them. Before, my conceited self would have wanted to write a "masterpiece" or something others might call literature. (Now I am ready to write a book that is as useful for propping up an uneven table leg as it is for being read.)

The Subject, after all, makes these lyrical devotions

meaningful. He is Meaning Itself. My words only find meaning as they huddle around Him.

I've been introducing songs in concert now for more than ten years. Some people complain about "all the talking." One famous speaker even said once, "Why can't Christian musicians shut up and just sing?" Yet most people would complain that I wasn't talking enough, that they'd like to hear more explanation of the songs I do. (I'm not sure whether that's a compliment or not.) It's hard in the course of a three-minute song to say everything you want to say about any subject, much less a subject like Jesus.

This book was born out of this frustration. It is wonderful to sing about Jesus, but there is so much more to tell. These essays are my opportunity to finally say all that I feel I need to say about the songs I've written so far on Jesus'

life, to finally get my thoughts off my chest for those who care enough to read.

I've divided the book into three sections, which correspond to the three divisions of Jesus' life: the Incarnation, the Ministry, and the Passion. The reflections in each section seek to give the background involved in the writing of each song (if it is relevant) as well as whatever biblical concepts are contained in it. These essays can be read straight through or at random. For some it might be helpful to listen to the music before or after you read the reflection. For others that might prove to be a distraction. I would encourage you to find your own strategy.

Please enjoy, but read with caution. Reading lyric is not the same as reading poetry. Good lyrics read like bad poetry. They are poems with a limp. They limp because they are without their main support and that is, of course, the music. Make up your own music as you go if you haven't heard or can't remember the original melodies.

In the end, I hope you come away with a deeper realization of who Jesus is, perhaps even of what He means. I pray that it has been made clear that these songs and essays are a reflection not of a mind that is perfectly devoted, but of one that longs to be so. They are reflections of a journey with Jesus that has been characterized often by failure, bitterness, even downright sinfulness.

If they prove to be helpful to someone who is in pain, it is because some pain was involved in writing them. If these reflections bring light, it is because their subject is the true Light. It has always been my prayer that the journey that is my walk with Christ will someday be characterized by joy. The thought that these words might bring someone the joy of knowing Jesus would be my greatest cause for rejoicing, next to the unspeakable joy of knowing Him!

---

*Contrary to academic and literary convention, all pronouns which refer to Jesus will be capitalized.

THE
INCARNATION

B*eyond all question
the mystery of
godliness is great ...
He appeared in a body.*

THE
INCARNATION

THE FINAL WORD

You and me we use so very many clumsy words.
The noise of what we often say is not worth being heard.
When the Father's Wisdom wanted to communicate His love,
He spoke it in one final perfect Word.

He spoke the Incarnation and then so was born the Son.
His final word was Jesus, He needed no other one.
Spoke flesh and blood so He could bleed and make a way Divine.
And so was born the baby who would die to make it mine.

And so the Father's fondest thought took on flesh and bone.
He spoke the living luminous Word, at once His will was done.
And so the transformation that in man had been unheard
Took place in God the Father as He spoke that final Word.

He spoke the Incarnation and then so was born the Son.
His final word was Jesus, He needed no other one.
Spoke flesh and blood so He could bleed and make a way Divine.
And so was born the baby who would die to make it mine.

And so the Light became alive
And manna became Man.
Eternity came into time
So we could understand.

He spoke the Incarnation and then so was born the Son.
His final word was Jesus, He needed no other one.
Spoke flesh and blood so He could bleed and make a way Divine.
And so was born the baby who would die to make it mine.*

---

*Hebrews 1:2.

E ven as I sit down to write this book a little voice inside my head is saying, "You can't do this, you'll never find the right words." It's a familiar voice. I've heard it before and will no doubt be hearing it the rest of my life. Who's to say whose voice it is? It may be the devil or one of his own, trying to defeat any small good that might come from the writing of this piece.

Perhaps it's a voice from the past, maybe a teacher long ago who once asked, "Can't you do anything right?" So now my mind continues to tell me the same negative thing. Maybe it's the voice of my older sister who, almost thirty years ago on a summer day as we sat in the hot car waiting for Mom, said, "You're the dumbest person in the whole family." And deep inside I was afraid she was right. And am afraid so still. Perhaps, in some way, it's all those voices at once, rallied against me, pushing for defeat. Who's to say?

Behind all those voices is one single, gentle Voice that says, "I believe you can do it." Though I have my doubts about all those other voices, I know whose voice this is. And so I write.

Finding the right words for a lyric doesn't seem as difficult to me as filling a page with prose. The structures of meter and rhyme have become so comfortable to me. The boundaries set by a melody seem almost like walls that protect the words. I have come to feel safe there. But to only have words! . . .

Almost everyone knows what it's like to struggle with those "clumsy bricks" we call words, from Thomas Jefferson, as he sought to define a new nation, to a schoolboy, as he tries to describe his summer vacation. All our words are only stuttering and stammering in comparison to that one final, perfect Word, the Word of God.

In the entire history of the human struggle with words, most of them have been expended trying to define, outline,

describe, and articulate that obvious and elusive, simple and complex, childlike and mysterious Word. The Word that is God, the Word that became flesh, the Word that is Wisdom. The Word we call Jesus.

To say that Jesus is the Word is another way of saying He is God speaking to us. While we struggle with our many "clumsy words," God needs only one Word to perfectly communicate the depth and mystery, the passion and the overwhelming grace of who He is. By that Word, Light became a living being. Manna became man. Wisdom became a person. In Him, Life came to life; all that God is came to us in that One Final Word we call Jesus.

My struggle to find words to describe Him is at the same time a struggle to find Him, I suppose. My mind would like to believe that if I could only somehow put together the right combination of words that someday I would find Him there at the end of them. But after all it is not a matter of words, as Paul says, but of power. [1]The Power is Jesus Himself. [2]Our struggle is really with Him, not with words. And like Jacob, who wrestled with God, I guess we will all find ourselves limping before it is all over.

THE PROMISE

The Lord God said when time was full
He would shine His light in the darkness.
He said a virgin would conceive*
And give birth to the Promise.
For a thousand years the dreamers dreamt
And hoped to see His love.
But the Promise showed their wildest dreams
Had simply not been wild enough.

The Promise was love.
And the Promise was life.
The Promise meant light to the world.
Living proof "Jehovah saves,"
For the name of the Promise was Jesus.

The Faithful One saw time was full
And the ancient pledge was honored.
So God the Son, the Incarnate One,
His final Word His own Son,
Was born in Bethlehem but came into our
Hearts to live.
What more could God have given, tell me
What more did He have to give?

The Promise was love.
And the Promise was life.
The Promise meant light to the world.
Living proof "Jehovah saves,"
For the name of the Promise was Jesus.

---

*Isaiah 7:14.

A long time ago I made a special promise to someone. For a number of reasons, some my fault and some not, I ended up breaking that promise. The feeling I felt afterward is impossible to describe. Remorse doesn't capture it. Nor does despair. The only way I can come close is to say I felt less a person after I broke that promise. I learned from that painful experience that when you make a real promise, a little bit of yourself goes along with it.

Promises are made with words. I might say, "I'll be there at three," or "I will never leave you." And that part of myself that goes with every promise is given to you through my words.

Our God is the great maker of promises. His Word, the Bible, is quite simply a collection of the promises He has made to us. In the beginning God told Adam and Eve, I will send someone who will crush the head of the serpent.[1] A promise. Most of the other promises in the Bible—if you look closely at them—are only a variation on that same theme. They concern Jesus, who would come to be known after all as the "Promised One." Through all these promises, God was trying to give something of Himself to Adam and to Israel—and finally to us. The Bible tells us that when the Promised One finally came, the Lord poured all of Himself into Him.

In the fullness of time what God had desired to do through the ages happened: He gave all of Himself to us through Jesus Christ, the Word of God, spoken at an incalculable price. When the Promised One appeared, God knew the giving of Jesus' life was in view. It makes you realize in the end what a costly thing it can be to make a promise. Sometimes it can even cost you your life!

IMMANUEL

A sign shall be given.
A virgin shall conceive.*
A human baby bearing
Undiminished Deity.
The glory of the nations,*
A light for all to see,
And hope for all who will embrace
This warm reality.

Immanuel.
Our God is with us.*
And if God is with us,
Who could stand against us?*
Our God is with us.
Immanuel.

For all those who live in the shadow of death
A glorious light has dawned.*
For all those who stumble in the darkness
Behold your Light has come!*

Immanuel.
Our God is with us.
And if God is with us,
Who could stand against us?
Our God is with us.
Immanuel.

So what shall be your answer?
Oh, will you hear the call
Of Him who did not spare His Son
But gave Him for us all?
On earth there is no power.
There is no depth or height

*That could ever separate us from the love
    of God in Christ.**

*Immanuel.
Our God is with us.
And if God is with us,
Who could stand against us?
Our God is with us.
Immanuel.*

We got married in December. Susan, my bride-to-be, had just finished finals, that day in fact. The church was already decorated for Christmas, and so we congratulated ourselves on saving money. In the nervousness, which most brides and grooms experience, I forgot much of what was said and done around us. When I see a picture of us together on that day, I honestly can't remember how I felt.

I do clearly remember the homily, however. With the promise of Christmas so close and our new life together just about to begin, our pastor, my dear friend Dr. Bill Lane, spoke a word of great power and promise. The word was *Immanuel:* "God with us."

For a couple looking at marriage in an era when fewer than fifty percent of marriages survive, *Immanuel* was a wonderful word to hear. It is, in fact, a wonderful word for anyone to hear, married or not, in this or any other time. For it means Jesus is with us every moment of every hour of every day of our lives.

**Isaiah 7:14; Psalm 96:3; Matthew 1:23; Romans 8:31; Isaiah 9:2; Isaiah 60:1; Romans 8:35.*

The implications of the name *Immanuel* are both comforting and unsettling. Comforting, because He has come to share the danger as well as the drudgery of our everyday lives. He desires to weep with us and to wipe away our tears. And what seems most bizarre, Jesus Christ, the Son of God, longs to share in and to be the source of the laughter and the joy we all too rarely know.

The implications are unsettling. It is one thing to claim that God looks down upon us, from a safe distance, and speaks to us (via long distance, we hope). But to say that He is right here, is to put ourselves and Him in a totally new situation. He is no longer the calm and benevolent observer in the sky, the kindly old caricature with the beard. His image becomes that of Jesus, who wept and laughed, who fasted and feasted, and who, above all, was fully present to those He loved. He was there with them. He is here with us.

Time and time again, both in sorrow and in joy, Susan

and I have become aware of His presence. As we looked into our new baby's face, bits and pieces of which reminded us of ourselves and our families, we knew the joyful sense of sharing that moment with Him. At a totally different time, in the middle of an argument, we've experienced His disturbing presence, which convicted us of failing to be to each other all He would want us to be.

Most incredible, however, are the times we know He is with us in the midst of our daily, routine lives. In the middle of cleaning the house or driving somewhere in the pickup, He stops us both in our tracks and makes His presence known. Often it's in the middle of the most mundane task that He lets us know He is there with us. We realize, then, that there can be no "ordinary" moments for people who live their lives with Jesus.

Jesus paid a tremendous price to be with us. Certainly the cross was the most obvious cost. But I believe more is in view.

We focus so much on the fact that Jesus died for us, we sometimes forget that He also lived for us and lives for us still. If Jesus had simply come as Himself, and not as one of us, the Bible makes it quite clear that we could not have borne the sight of His presence, anymore than Moses could have looked directly at the face of God.

Imagine what it would be like to be at the Father's side one moment and struggling to sleep in a cattle trough the next. Imagine what it would be like to go from hearing the praise of angels to suffering the taunts of stupid men. The cost to Jesus is an indication of the incredible value of what He came to give us. And because no one will ever fully know what that cost Jesus, we can only begin to understand the incredible value of His gift to us.

The apostle Paul realized the indescribable gift of Immanuel in a passage which many consider the height of his inspiration. He concludes, "If God is for us, who could be

against us?" God is on our side, right or wrong, because even when we are wrong, He still loves us.

"Never will I leave you, never will I forsake you," Jesus says. That is what Bill was trying to tell us on that first day of our life together. Immanuel. God is with you, now and forever.

On that cold and nervous day in December, no better name could have been spoken to Susan and me. And in seven years of marriage the truth of it means more to us now than we could have ever imagined!

TO THE MYSTERY

When the Father longed to show
A love He wanted us to know,
He sent His only Son and so
Became a holy embryo.

That is the Mystery!
More than you can see.
Give up on your pondering
And fall down on your knees.

No fiction as fantastic and wild
A mother made by her own child.
The hopeless babe who cried
Was God Incarnate and man deified.

That is the Mystery!
More than you can see.
Give up on your pondering
And fall down on your knees.

Because the fall did devastate
Creator must now re-create.
And so to take our sin
Was made like us so we could be like Him.

That is the Mystery!
More than you can see.
Give up on your pondering
And fall down on your knees.

I used to think that mysteries existed only to be solved, like a Dorothy Sayers' novel. It may have been the result of living in a scientific age. Or more likely it was the presumption of my own fallenness. Like so many others today, I actually believed I had the ability to understand it all, given enough time to figure things out. When I heard someone refer to the "mystery" of Christ, I assumed that Christ was only a mystery to nonbelievers. Yet the Mystery of Christ is reserved only for those who do believe. To "know" the Mystery of Christ is to realize that it is indeed just that, a mystery.

To represent faith in Jesus merely as something we come to understand and accept is to rob it of the mystery of being in relationship with something that is infinitely bigger and wiser than we are. His ways are not our ways, the prophet Isaiah tells us, and that hasn't changed.[1] He is still the Creator and we, His creatures. Like the birds, we receive our daily bread from His hand and each breath of life as His gracious gift. Is that not itself a mystery?

Mystery is not a category only for the spiritually elite, secret knowledge reserved for the members of the "deeper life club." The mysteries of faith in Christ are for everyone who claims to be in relationship with Him. The basic truths of Christianity are mysteries, not understandable, not "our ways": the virgin birth of Jesus, the Trinity, grace, prayer, the union of the believer with Christ, the Cross, and perhaps most mysterious, and key to them all, the Incarnation.

A simple man, a carpenter from obscure Galilee, was not merely the representative of, but was God incarnate and man deified, "very God of very God," as the creed says. The Infinite contained in the ridiculously finite. Is *anyone* willing to raise his/her hand and say, "I understand"?

So what is our condition, then? Are we irrationalists, left to stumble about, blind, in the dark? Is that the purpose of mystery? Nothing could be farther from the truth. The

purpose of the mystery of Christ is not to blind our eyes but to open them to belief in Him. The purpose is not to separate us into the "spiritual" and the "worldly," but to make us one as we try to live the mystery. In fact it is the substance of the mystery that makes possible the only true "knowing."

We are not irrationalists, we are believers. Only by believing do we "know." We do not claim to fully understand the mystery. Not in the least, or else it would be no mystery. It is because of the mystery, and not in spite of it, that we know. The mystery calls forth faith, giving us the ability to "know" with the heart as well as the mind. Even the knowing is a mystery.

CARMEN CHRISTI

Who being in very nature God
Would not grasp equality with Him
But made Himself nothing
And took up a servant's nature.

Made in human likeness.
Found in appearance as man.
He humbled Himself, was obedient,
Even to death on a cross.

At Jesus' name every knee shall bow
In heaven and in all the earth.
To the Father's glory each tongue cry,
"Jesus is Lord!"

And so He has been exalted
By God to the highest place.
And given a name as exalted
Above every other name.

At Jesus' name every knee shall bow
In heaven and in all the earth.
To the Father's glory each tongue cry,
"Jesus is Lord!"*

---

*Philippians 2:6–11.

35

The Emperor Trajan had been waiting for a report about the troublesome sect called Christians from one of his spies named Pliny the Younger. When the report finally did come, the emperor was disappointed by its brevity and lack of accusations: "They worship one Christ, whom they revere as God."[1]

Pliny's brief report also claimed that the Christians "gather early in the morning and sing a hymn" to this Christ whom they worship. Many scholars believe that this is the hymn found in Philippians 2:6~11, which has come to be known as the "Carmen Christi," or "Hymn to Christ."

Earlier Roman reports had confused the name "Christos," or Christ, for "Chrestus," which was a common personal name given to a slave.[2] It was an honest mistake and an understandable one, considering the reputation of the Galilean carpenter who acted more like a slave than an anointed king.

I find it touching that before this passage was ever made the topic of theological debate, it was a simple hymn. Before it was preached, it was sung. Without reasoning and argumentation the early believers embraced these complex incarnational truths by means of a simple melody.

"When the soul hears music it lets down its best guard," Socrates said. And so with music those early saints sang their way to a belief in the unbelievable. With their hearts as well as their minds, they embraced the mystery of the Incarnation of Jesus. It was a simple song, with only one verse and a chorus. Let's look at the verse first:

> Who, being in very nature God,
>   did not consider equality with God
>   something to be grasped,
>   but *made Himself nothing*,
>   taking the very nature of *a servant*,
>   being made in human likeness.

And being found in appearance as a
man,
He *humbled Himself*
and became *obedient* to death—
even death on a cross![3]

In the verse two concepts which were central in the life
of Jesus were presented: humility and servanthood. Jesus
"made Himself nothing" and "humbled Himself," the early
Christians sang. He took the form of a servant, though He
might have grasped equality with God. This was the puzzling nature of the appearance of "God with us." In humility and as a servant, He came to live and die for us. God
held up Jesus to us and said, "This is what it means to be
created in My image!" Who would have ever dreamt the
image would be that of a servant?

The verse closed with a focal theme, the concept of obedience: "He humbled Himself and became obedient to
death—even death on a cross." This characteristic becomes
a lens through which the traits of humility and servanthood
become focused in a surprising way. It was the "twist" to
the lyric that every good writer goes for. "He became obedient," the verse says as it comes to a close. Not just obedience as an abstract concept but vividly and radically
portrayed in flesh and blood. Death on the cross! It is no
longer appropriate to refer to simple obedience. From this
point on we are talking about "radical" obedience, which
will transform everything, both for Jesus and for us.

After the single verse comes the chorus:

Therefore God exalted Him to the highest place
and gave Him the name that is above every name,
that at the name of Jesus every knee should bow,
   in heaven and on earth and under the earth,
and every tongue confess that Jesus Christ is Lord,
to the glory of God the Father.[4]

The chorus of this early hymn must have resolved from a minor to a major key. I hear sopranos screeching and baritones giving it everything they've got. In the back someone breaks out the tambourine. The song "takes off"!

In the chorus the concepts of the verse are transformed from humility to exaltation and from servanthood to Lordship. It is called "radical reversal." The chorus opens with a telling "therefore," which points to the connection between the two pairs of concepts. Observe the radical reversal from the One who refused glory and "made Himself nothing" to One who is exalted to the highest place! Remember the One who took upon Himself the form of a servant? Now every tongue confesses that same person as Lord. Every knee is bowed before Him as well. Jesus Christ is Lord!

This ancient song paints a wonderful picture of the Incarnation of Christ and of a powerful process that is at work in the world. With one dark verse and one brilliant chorus, we see Jesus and ourselves in a new light. The

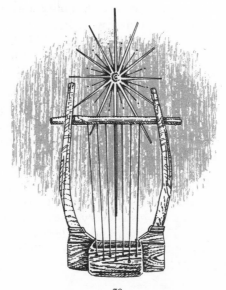

apostle Paul was giving the Philippian Christians more than a picture of Christ. He was suggesting servanthood and radical obedience as a pattern for their lives—and for ours.

Paul made his point clear by one simple introductory phrase in verse 5: "Your attitude should be the same as that of Christ Jesus." Jesus' life demonstrated what it meant for us to be created in God's image, (or rather re-created, since re-creating is what we needed).

As we sing to the glory of Christ we are changed into His image. Humble servants who through our obedience will someday be glorified and exalted, for Jesus promised, "He who humbles himself will be exalted."[5] And "Whoever desires to become great among you, let him be your servant."[6] That process, which was so powerfully seen in the life of Jesus, is at work in our own lives as well! The way is humility, servanthood, and radical obedience; people like the Emperor Trajan and Pliny and so many in our own day can never understand.

JOSEPH'S SONG

"How could it be?
This baby in my arms,
Sleeping now so peacefully,
'The Son of God,' the angel said.
How could it be?

"Lord, I know He's not my own,
Not of my flesh, not of my bone.
Still Father let this baby be
The son of my love.

"Father, show me where I fit into
This plan of yours.
How can a man be father to the Son of God?
Lord, for all my life I've been a simple carpenter.
How can I raise a king?
How can I raise a king?

"He looks so small,
His face and hands so fair.
And when He cries the sun just seems to disappear,
But when He laughs
It shines again.
How could it be?

"Father, show me where I fit into
This plan of yours.
How can a man be father to the Son of God?
Lord, for all my life I've been a simple carpenter.
How can I raise a king?
How can I raise a king?

How could it be?
This baby in my arms,
Sleeping now so peacefully,

'The Son of God,' the angel said.
How could it be?"

Asimple carpenter stands in the shadow of the stable, in the shadow of history. People come and go.
The shepherds have seen angels. The Magi, a star.
Others have only heard fantastic rumors. Some of them
have come hundreds of miles. Some only across the street.
The silent figure stands there watching them come and go,
the weeping ones who adore and the curious ones who
merely gape. He is the gentle foster-father of Jesus, a rural
carpenter named Joseph.

The best in him rejoices with the others. God has finally
come to His people! The worst in him still wonders if he
isn't the biggest fool in Bethlehem tonight.

Joseph was the first person to really struggle with the
Incarnation. Mary's momentary, "How could these things
be?" seemed to come and go, like a cool breeze. But Joseph saw no angels. He only dreamed dreams. He had no
quickening in his belly to tell him that life had indeed been
conceived without his flesh. We know almost nothing about
Joseph, apart from his gentleness and willingness to say
"No" to himself for Mary's sake and for God's.

Imagine the dilemma of that simple man, finding himself cast in the role of father to the Son of God. Though
that beautiful infant was not part of his body, the baby
must have quickly taken over Joseph's heart, as most
adopted children have a way of doing. As he held that
squirming bundle in his arms, Joseph must have asked the
question every new father asks himself and God, "How
could it be?"

I first heard that question when my older brother held his son for the first time. I asked myself the same question a few years later when our first daughter, Katherine, was born. It is a question for which there is no answer. We really don't expect one. Joseph probably didn't expect an answer either.

It is an impossible task, being a parent. Not just difficult . . . impossible. To take a life from its first breath on through to maturity—to feed, clothe, educate, and all the rest. How could it be?

God is the giver of such impossible tasks. He says to one-hundred-year-old Abraham and ninety-year-old Sarah, "Make a baby!" He tells a young virgin, "You are with child." He informs a young, confused carpenter, who has never so much as touched his bride-to-be, "You are a father!" Perhaps, in the end, it's not our abilities, but simply the fact that He says so. It is not a matter of what we can or cannot do but of God's power.

So now Joseph (who is also by the way, a virgin) is a father. His task, along with the already impossible task of fatherhood? To be father to the Son of God!

How did Joseph do? We regretfully have no scenes of him with Jesus in the carpenter shop. But since Jesus was also known as a carpenter, He must have learned His trade somewhere, and why not from Joseph? We know for certain that Jesus made it to manhood with a wonderfully strong and simple vision of what *father* meant. He must have learned it at least in part from Joseph. Before He shrieked, "Abba!" with a man's tormented voice in the garden of Gethsemane, He must have tenderly called out that same name in an innocent child's voice to that man in the shadows, Joseph.

CELEBRATE THE CHILD

Celebrate the Child who is the Light.
Now the darkness is over.
No more wandering in the night.
Celebrate the Child who is the Light.

You know this is no fable;
Godhead and manhood became one.
We see He's more than able,
And so we live to God the Son.

Celebrate the Child who is the Light.
Now the darkness is over.
No more wandering in the night.
Celebrate the Child who is the Light.

Firstborn of creation,*
Lamb and Lion, God and Man.
The Author of Salvation.
Almighty wrapped in swaddling bands.

Celebrate the Child who is the Light.
Now the darkness is over.
No more wandering in the night.
Celebrate the Child who is the Light.

*Colossians 1:15.

Christmas is a struggle for my wife and me. Our ongoing war with the world seems to intensify as the decorations go up all over town. There is His name, in every window. Sometimes there is even a statue of His sweet infant body, lying in some straw with shepherds and wise men standing around with blank porcelain expressions. (I've always thought their faces convey the attitude of the world toward Christmas: blank, dazed, and bewildered.) If people today would just look at the birth of Jesus "straight on," they would be puzzled that we should celebrate the horrific birth of a baby who was born to die. The contradictions should be more than the world can take. If Christianity could just be seen for what it is—a paradox and a mystery. The beginning in that dirty stable is one of the greatest mysteries: the plainness and the greatness of Jesus, the grime and the glory. Wise men with gold in their hands and shepherds with sheep dung on their shoes. A smelly stable below and a shining star above. The birth of a gentle Lamb who was the fiercest Lion.

But the world doesn't seem to struggle with these contradictions. They join in our season of celebration unruffled and oftentimes more joyful than we.

In an attempt to preserve some of this perspective, it is our family tradition to pile in the car and go to a real working barn, with horses in their stalls and a barn cat on the prowl for its prey amongst the hay bales. Together, we read the Christmas story by candlelight. The odor and the dark seem to press in against the fragile light of our candle. The horses stamp their feet against the cold and look at us sideways, as horses must, as if we were a little "off" for being there in the middle of the night.

The shabbiness of this setting reminds us of that other shabby place Jesus chooses everyday to be born: the human heart, a place more filthy and cold than any stable. All this comes so much closer to reality for us than the singing

Christmas trees or the huge services. They may have their place and might become a genuine part of the real celebration, but not without the smell of the straw and the bewildered animals who seem almost about to speak. A baby and a barn. Only with these things can the celebration be truly complete.

If Christmas means anything to you, then it must mean everything. It is a beginning and an end. It is a time of darkness and inexpressible light. It is a time of blessed relief at finally seeing all God's promises come true in one person. It is a time of tension as well as we look ahead in the life of this dear little one with a kind of historical omnipresence because we know how it all will end, on earth anyway. As our family gathers around our faint, flickering candle to read the Christmas story, the loneliness of the stable reminds us of the loneliness of another place on a hill outside Jerusalem. The rough trough seems almost as cruel a place as a cross. The infant cries we hear coming from

the stable seem no less desperate than His final cry, and no less forsaken.

Celebrate? you say. Yes, most heartily, amidst the dung of the stable, which is, of course, the refuse of the world. Celebrate at the foot of that ghastly cross because it is the hope of the world. Gather around a cattle trough and celebrate a baby born in poverty and rejected because He is the Savior of the world!

LONG, LONG JOURNEY

It was such a long, long journey,
Looking for the Holy Child.
So many times we thought the signs had lied
Till in Nazareth we found the Boy,
Just as He had started walking.
A child so fair we hardly could believe.

The prophets told us He'd be coming,
But we never did believe
Until we saw the star of Jacob in the east,
Shedding light upon our way,
Shining brighter than the moon
Above a simple house in Galilee.

Just like any little boy
He was always on the move,
And into everything that He could find.
But the look upon His face
As we offered Him our gifts
Made us know for certain Jesus was a king.

The prophets told us He'd be coming,
But we never did believe
Until we saw the star of Jacob in the east,
Shedding light upon our way,
Shining brighter than the moon
Above a simple house in Galilee.

I've always identified with the wise men. Not because I'm particularly wise, but because I've always wanted to be. I used to see wisdom as something to possess, as a commodity, a "thing." I suppose that's why I went to college to study philosophy. There was a hunger in me to know, to possess, something hard, if not impossible, to define. For the lack of a better term I called it *wisdom*.

Thankfully, early in those college years I began to discover that there was more to wisdom than the accumulation of facts and information. Although I hadn't found out what true wisdom was as yet, at least I was given the grace to recognize its impostor.

Wisdom is not the ability to be correct all the time, although I suppose people who are wise are right more often than people who are stupid. Now I've learned that wisdom is not facts or the accumulation of them, though that is what our educational system seems to believe.

Genuine wisdom is concerned with life, a life well-lived, perhaps. Wisdom isn't something we know as much as something we become. Like life, wisdom is impossible to define or grasp. If the Magi were truly "wise men," they must have understood this. Perhaps that's why they left on their long journey in the first place.

It was a long, long journey. They came "from the east." Scholars think they might have been priests of Zoroaster, probably from Persia. They foolishly followed Jacob's star for months, perhaps even years, which doesn't sound like wisdom to me but rather foolishness or faith.

They are called "Magi" in the Gospels. Herodotus described the Magi as a special group of priests who had to be present at sacrifices to speak certain "sacred words," known only to them. When we finally come upon the Magi in Matthew, however, they don't seem to have much to say.

The Bible simply says they "bowed down and worshiped Him." Perhaps they were silent because they recog-

nized in this little baby a Wisdom that went beyond their stammering words. Instead of pondering the mystery of this Wisdom, they fell on their knees and worshiped. They must have felt great relief at coming to the end of their long journey, for there is no true worship without that sense that you have finally found what you've been looking for all your life.

We assume there were three wise men because three gifts are mentioned. I'd like to think there were many more. They offered the baby gifts that were no doubt intended for some potentate: gold, frankincense, and myrrh. Upon seeing the young child (by now, Jesus was no longer a baby and the holy family was living in a house) the Magi's "priceless" gifts must have shrunk into worthless insignificance as they watched the toddler playing with gold, which meant nothing to Him and indeed never would.

It had been a long journey. For many of us it is a long journey still. The great writer Frederick Buechner described his life as a journey, a sacred one. So did C. S. Lewis, Malcolm Muggeridge, and others. Bunyan's famous metaphor of the Pilgrim's Progress is really only the story of a journey.

Our journey begins where the wise men's ended. Like them, we have found a Wisdom not to ponder but to worship, a wisdom that is not a matter of words but who is the Word. This Wisdom has everything to do with life because He is the Life. He gives us Wisdom because He gives us Himself. The Magi journeyed to Jesus, but our journey is *with* Jesus, a sacred and a long, long journey.

NOW THAT I'VE HELD
HIM IN MY ARMS

An old man in the temple,
Waiting in the court,
Waiting for the answer to a promise,
And all at once he sees them
In the morning sunshine
A couple coming carrying a baby.

"Now that I've held Him in my arms
My life can come to an end.
Let Your servant now depart in peace.
I've seen Your salvation.
He's the Light of the Gentiles,
And the glory of His people Israel."

Mary and the baby come.
And in her hand five shekels,
The price to redeem her baby boy.
The baby softly cooing,
Nestled in her arms.
Simeon takes the boy and starts to sing.

"Now that I've held Him in my arms
My life can come to an end.
Let Your servant now depart in peace.
I've seen Your salvation.
He's the Light of the Gentiles,
And the glory of His people Israel."

And now's the time to take Him in your arms.
Your life will never come to an end.
He's the only way that you'll find peace.
He'll give you salvation.

He's the Light of the Gentiles,
*And the glory of His people Israel.**

This lyric has always been my mother's favorite. She
cries every time she hears it as the various pictures
contained in the words flash across her sentimental
mind. It used to puzzle me that her favorite song should be
one that causes her to cry until I realized that it also was a
song about someone holding a baby, her favorite thing in
the world to do (along with crying, that is). And so the
song is her favorite.

I suppose it's one of my favorites as well. Certainly I
enjoy holding babies, especially my own, and would probably enjoy crying the way my mother does if only I could
bring myself to tears more easily. Yet this song is special to
me for another reason. It describes how before Jesus was
born, waiting was the greatest part of faith. It speaks of the
power a promise can have. Each time I think about Simeon
a new truth seems to come to the surface.

Simeon was an old man when he received a very special promise from God. The promise? You will not die until
you have seen the coming of the Messiah. For an elderly
Jew and a man of faith, there was no greater promise. It
became the nexus of his whole life. From that time on, Simeon spent the remainder of his days waiting, as did all the
faithful who lived before the advent of Jesus. Having faith
meant waiting for God to keep His promise. Abraham.
Moses. The prophets. All those who trusted God demonstrated their faith by their ability to wait. So Simeon waited

Luke 2:22-35.

in the temple for God to make good on His fantastic promise.

We really don't know what Simeon was expecting, though we can guess. Perhaps he was looking for a king who would come in great glory, since that was the image of "Messiah" for many of his friends. Perhaps as he sat in the temple court, Simeon kept his eyes focused on the sky, waiting for the clouds to part and reveal a great and glorious king. Each sunbeam that broke through might be a sign that the promise was about to come true.

Perhaps Simeon was expecting a warrior. Many were hoping the Messiah would be a warlike leader, especially a group of radicals known as the zealots. (One or two of Jesus' own disciples had belonged to this group.) They saw the Messiah as someone who would kill the Romans. Of course, Jesus offered them a blood bath of sorts, only it was His own blood, not anyone else's.

We do not know what Simeon was expecting, but we do know what he got. A little baby wrapped in rags, with paupers for parents. Jesus. A most unlikely person to change the world. Yet there is hardly anyone who could imagine what this world would be like if He had not come, even an unbeliever.

There the Holy Baby was, cradled in His mother's arms. What must have gone through Simeon's mind when God pointed out His Promised One. "There He is, the one with the dirty diaper." Simeon was wise enough to expect the unexpected from the Lord. He went straight to Joseph and Mary. Luke gives us the wonderful detail that he took Jesus and held Him in his arms. That, for me, is one of the most significant moments of the nativity narratives. In this one simple man two worlds meet.

The Old Testament embraces the New. For what is the Old Testament but a collection of promises? God promised Adam and Eve, I will send someone to crush the head of

the serpent.¹ Now that One had come. As Simeon took Him into his arms he responded poetically, perhaps even in a song, as Adam had first responded to Eve, as Mary had responded to the angel. The promise had become flesh. It was "the good news."

It was good news to finally be able to embrace the Promised One. But far and away the best news of all is that He embraces us. That was the reason for His coming. Most of us describe our coming to faith by saying, "I've asked Jesus into my life." We should really say He has invited us into His life!

That was the reason for Simeon's song. Deep inside his tired old heart, he knew that the infant he held in his arms was in truth the One who had been holding him all his life long.

SPIRIT OF THE AGE

I thought that I heard crying,
Coming through my door.
Was it Rachel weeping for her sons
Who were no more?
Could it have been the babies,
Crying for themselves,
Never understanding that they died
For someone else?

A voice is heard of weeping and of wailing.*
History speaks of it on every page,
Of innocent and helpless little babies,
Offerings to the spirit of the age.

No way of understanding
This sad and painful sign.
Whenever Satan rears his head
There comes a tragic time.
If he could crush the cradle,
Then that would stop the cross.
He knew that once the Light was born
His every hope was lost.*

A voice is heard of weeping and of wailing;
History speaks of it on every page,
Of innocent and helpless little babies,
Offerings to the spirit of the age.

Now, every age has heard it;
That voice that speaks from hell:
"Sacrifice your children,
And for you it will be well."
The subtle serpent's lying,

*Jeremiah 31:15; Revelation 12:1–4; Romans 16:20.

His dark and ruthless rage.
Behold, it is revealed to be
The spirit of the age.

A voice is heard of weeping and of wailing.
History speaks of it on every page,
Of innocent and helpless little babies,
Offerings to the spirit of the age.

Soon all the ones who seemed
To die for nothing
Will stand beside the Ancient of Days.
With joy we'll see that Infant
From the manger
Come and crush the spirit of the age. *

The line was all too long. The Israelites were waiting with the pagan worshipers, all holding their babies. Some of the infants were crying, others smiling and playing with their dazed parents. All the while the priests of Molech were busily stoking their furnace-god.

The large bronze idol was shaped like a man. It was really nothing more than a huge furnace into which the priests were piling wood. The lower part of the idol was already glowing white hot. Its arms were upraised, forming a ramp into its flaming belly. The worshipers of Molech were rolling their helpless babies down this ramp. Precious, innocent life was being offered up to a demonic spirit, "the spirit of the age." The line was so pitifully long.

A thousand years later we can see another sinister line. A line of soldiers. Their orders from Herod read: "Kill all

---

Matthew 2:16.

male babies in Bethlehem two years old and younger." The purpose of the order was to snuff out the life of a new "king of the Jews." The dazed look on the soldiers' faces was not unlike the blank stare of those other Israelites, so long ago. For after all, they were really standing in the same pitifully long line.

Along with the weeping that followed the slaughter of the innocents, Matthew could hear the words of Jeremiah, the prophet of the painful exile who knew more about weeping than any of us. "A voice is heard in Ramah, mourning and great weeping, Rachel weeping for her children and refusing to be comforted, because her children are no more."[1]

We can trace this dark, grim line down to our own present day. Today it forms not before pagan idols or bloodthirsty tyrants but in front of "clinics," where the innocent and not-so-innocent come for "help." Again the innocents are offered to "the spirit of the age."

People who have gotten out of satanic cults tell us that the most coveted sacrifice today is still an innocent baby. It seems the greater the innocence of the victim, the greater the power of the offering. Through scores of innocent infant sacrifices, Satan has sought such power, but in vain. For just as crucial as the innocence of the victim is its willingness to be offered.

There was a victim once who was completely innocent and totally willing to be offered as a sacrifice. His innocence was that of a child even though He was a grown man. He was willing, not because He desired power but because He wanted to be obedient to His Father. His sacrifice is unique, once for all. He alone had the power to break that long, dark line. And He did.

Sooner than any of us think, He will return with all those innocents who seemed to die for nothing. The Bible says, those who believe in Him will "marvel" at His Com-

ing.[2] That long, pitiful line will finally come to an end. And those who stood in the dark, grim line through the centuries will find themselves standing in another line, even darker still.

LULLABY FOR JESUS

Baby Jesus, please don't cry.
Now let me wipe the tears from Your eyes.
You cry as though Your heart would break.
Please don't spend Your first night awake.

Shepherds 'round You mean no harm.
They long to hold You in their arms.
To cradle as they might a lamb,
But You're too small to understand.

Cattle lowing long to sing
A lullaby to soothe the King.
A cry so full of pain and fright
That pierces through the lonely night.

Baby Jesus, please don't weep.
It's night and time for You to sleep.
The stars that shine don't match the glow
Of all the ones who'll come to know.

This baby sleeping in the hay,
The Son of God who's come to save,
The Light, the only Way that's true,
Who'll die upon a cross for you.

I had just finished giving a talk on the poverty of the nativity of Jesus to a group at a small country church when one sweet lady walked up to me. I could tell by her expression that she was bothered by some of the things I had said and that her "guns were loaded." I braced myself.

"I simply do not agree with your picture of the birth of Jesus, young man!"

"What exactly troubles you about it?" I asked.

"Well," she paused as she searched for the right words, "I don't believe He cried the way you said."

I gently pressed her to show me a passage from the Bible that would lead her to believe such a thing. She thought for a while and couldn't come up with anything. Finally, out of desperation, I suppose, she retorted, "Well, what about 'Silent Night, Holy Night'?"

That dear sister is only an extreme example of a tendency we all have to incorporate our traditions into Scripture. We sing "Away in a Manger" and believe what we sing: "No crying He makes." So He must not have cried.

We thereby dismiss the examples we see every day from a multitude of newborns. I wonder if, way back in our minds, we believe He never soiled a diaper!

We celebrate the birth of Jesus in December, so we sprinkle snow on our nativity scenes and sermonize about Joseph and Mary's struggle with the cold. In truth, the Bible says nothing about the season, apart from a reference to the fact that the shepherds were "keeping watch" in the fields all through the night, which might mean it was the season when lambs were being born, the only time shepherds stay in the fields all night. If that is so, Jesus was probably born in the spring. I'd like to think it was April, since that is the month of my own birthday!

These false images of the Nativity have provided the foundation for a distorted picture of Jesus' entire life,

which simply must go if we are to try to grasp the real picture, given in the Gospels, of the nativity of Jesus.

We know from Scripture that Jesus wept as a man. It is naive to think He did not cry as a baby. Tears are a basic part of what it means to be human. It is one of the sad signs of our fallen world that the first sign we give to show that we're alive is a cry. It was to this fallen world that Jesus came, not an imaginary one without tears. For the "Man of Sorrows" it would seem that tears were an even more integral part of His life than ours. He came as much to weep for us as to die for us.

My response to this realization of the weeping baby Jesus was to write Him a lullaby. It seemed only natural. For me it was a way of coming closer to His birth, to feel the darkness of that night, to smell the smells of the stable, and to hear that fragile newborn voice crying out in the night to His mother, Mary, and in a way, to me as well.

THE GIFT

Forgive me, oh Lord,
For being so dim.
I've embraced all Your gifts,
Put my arms around them.
I was holding so tight;
It was all I could do.
I forgot that my arms
Belong just around You.

Now Jesus has taught
To let everything go.
All the things that you own.
All the people you know.
If you stop asking questions
And simply obey,
You'll possess them in a much
More beautiful way.

Yesterday was Christmas. We packed up the kids and went to my parents' house for the ceremonial opening of gifts. As usual there were enough presents piled under the tree for fifty people instead of fifteen. The orgy of unwrapping went on as it always does, and as I'm sure it did in millions of other homes as well.

It was the first Christmas our three-year-old, Kate, was aware of gifts. Her little face lit up when her "pile" was pointed out to her. Still she tore into her presents like an old veteran. There were dolls, of course, and clothes family members had given her. Her grandmother had made a dollhouse for her. That was the "special" gift this year.

When Kate was finished opening her things, she was allowed to open her little brother's presents for him, since he is only a year old and couldn't care less about presents. For him the fun apparently was having all the people around him and getting all the attention (since he is the baby of the family for now). He hasn't learned the place of presents in Christmas. Maybe he's better off.

After Kate was finished with his presents, she went on to open every other present she could get her little hands on and had to be stopped before she ripped open every box as well. This brought a flood of tears and angry protests, "No! Mine!" There are barely two years between Kate and her little brother, Will, but they are centuries apart in their reaction to Christmas and presents. I wonder if most of us still don't need to learn the place of presents in Christmas?

There is nothing wrong with gifts. God Himself is happy to give us gifts. You can hardly open your eyes without seeing one of them. Every breath, each moment of life, can be seen as a gift from this marvelous Giver. The trouble comes when we forget the distinction between the gifts and the giver. Let me give you an example.

My wife gave me a book this Christmas, one I had wanted for a long time. It was a rather obscure book on

N. C. Wyeth, which had to be special ordered. When I discovered it (she had tried to hide it in the wardrobe) I was surprised and so happy. I didn't hug the book, however, and give it a big sloppy kiss. No, I dropped the book and embraced her, the one who had given such a special gift. As wonderful as the present was, it was she, Susan, who had gone to the trouble of special ordering it. As long as we reserve our thanksgiving and embraces for our loved ones, and not the gifts they give, we'll be closer to what Christmas is really all about.

I believe the same holds true when it comes to our relationship with that greatest of Givers. The temptation to foolishly embrace His gifts is greater because they are infinitely better and more beautiful. Creation with all its beauty. The "stars that do shine" and the rest of the world around us have all been "embraced" by different groups as idols to worship. After all, they are beautiful gifts. But their beauty is only a shadow of His beauty. And if embracing them gives a certain joy (and we must confess that it does) how much more joy would come from embracing Him!

Perhaps we are tempted to embrace God's gifts because we really desire to possess them. Like Kate, clutching her father's copy of N. C. Wyeth and saying "No! Mine!" we desire to possess things we really cannot either understand or possess. Even the gift of life, something all of us cling to with both hands, cannot be possessed. God gives us fantastic gifts, but He wants us to remember that everything belongs to Him. He wants to be our only possession.

A CHRISTMAS SONG

The Light of the World
Contained in a baby
Smiling so bright as He lay in the hay.
Begotten of God,
The Son of the Father,
Veiled in the flesh of a babe.

But how could this be?
A child in a manger,
A place only fit for the cattle to feed.
A birth so despised.
But it's just the beginning
For a Man of Sorrows He'll be.

The hard-hearted men
Slam doors in the darkness.
They wouldn't make room but in these days, do we?
The forces so dark
Tried so hard to kill it,
But nothing could darken the Light that was born.

A new age has come
For God is among us
Veiled in the flesh of a babe.

THE
MINISTRY

H*e will be a stone that causes men to stumble and a rock that makes them fall.*

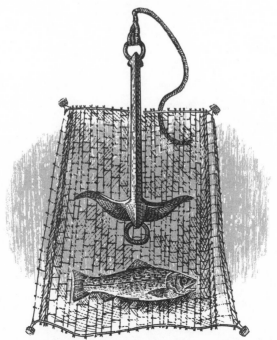

THE
MINISTRY

THE VOICE OF THE CHILD

I am an old rabbi.
Where's the Child who was here only yesterday?
How my heart started to beat as I sat at His feet!
For the things He'd say.
The questions I asked Him had weighed on my mind
An eternity.
But the self-righteous show I had made my disguise,
Started to slip as I looked in His eyes.
But rather than stay, for my pride's sake
I walked away.

Come listen awhile to the voice of the Child.
Stand in awe of the Wisdom of God.
Hear what He has to say,
For the time is today.
You can come or just walk away.

Then late in the night
I awoke to a voice deep inside of me.
It was gentle and mild,
Like the voice of the Child my mind's eye could see.
It spoke of the promises made to my people through Abraham.
And at once all the prophecy made sense to me.
I'd studied them so long, why couldn't I see?
In one holy moment I knew the Messiah was He.

Come listen awhile to the voice of the Child.
Stand in awe of the Wisdom of God.
Hear what He has to say,
For the time is today.
You can come or just walk away.

I am an old rabbi.
Where's the Child who was here only yesterday?

How my heart started to beat as I sat at His feet!
Oh, the things He'd say.
I've just got to find Him and tell Him I'm sorry
I walked away.

Most of us are already well on our way to becoming whatever it is we're going to be by the time we're thirty. In a large part, the story of our lives is the story of those years. During that time we receive whatever education we're probably going to get. We fall in love for the first, and hopefully the last time, and many of us marry by then. During those first three decades we set a course for our lives, the course which most of us will follow until we die.

By the time I was thirty I had been a Christian for twenty-two years. I was finished with college and had the last degree I would ever earn. I had been married to my wife, Susan, for four years and our first child, Katherine, had already come into the world. The ministry of teaching and music to which I had been called was well underway. I was basically "me," the person I'll probably be till the day I die, for better or for worse.

In that block of time, in that story which is uniquely my story, the most important event had already taken place by the time I was only eight years old. During a Sunday morning service I gave my life to Jesus and He gave His Life to me. I struggle today to find the words to describe just what happened. The best I can do is say I met Him that day and realized that His extravagant demonstration of love on the cross was for me. I've wondered ever since how anyone could walk away from such a love as that.

The Gospels are hopelessly silent about the first thirty years of Jesus' life. They are often referred to as the "silent period." The New Testament gives us only one precious window through which we can look into that secret childhood. It is frustratingly brief and leaves us longing for more detail. . . .

Jesus was only twelve. His parents always came to Jerusalem for the Feast of Passover. Whether they always took Him along or not we do not know. Nor do we know if the Passover meal had a particular impact on the young boy, if it made Him weep or become thoughtful. The one thing we do learn is that Jesus' parents lost Him! Imagine, having been entrusted with raising the Messiah, only to lose Him. Not for a few moments but for three days!

When Mary and Joseph finally found Jesus, He was in the temple, where He said they should have looked in the first place. He was with the teachers, the same group He would come into conflict with so often as a man. We have no indication of the tone of His discussion with them. Was He dumbfounding them with His innate wisdom? Was He asking simple, but unanswerable, questions to confound them? Luke tells us that those who heard were "amazed at his understanding and his answers."[1] Were the teachers amazed by a precocious boy or by someone who was infinitely more?

While the teachers were amazed, Luke tells us Joseph and Mary were "astonished." Mary gently asked, "Why have you treated us like this? Your father and I have been anxiously searching for you."[2]

Jesus almost always answered a question with another question. And this incident was no exception. He could not understand why they would have looked anywhere else but in the temple, His "Father's house." Even as He was misunderstood all His life so His own parents fail to understand what He means.

In the face of such a hopeless lack of detail we are left to our own imaginations to take our place alongside the teachers and listen to that small voice speak as no one had ever spoken before. One seemingly naive word of His might have exposed the hypocrisy of a Pharisee, something He specialized in later on. Another moment His childlike words might have comforted the confused and weary hopes of a scribe who had longed to see the day he now saw. Chances are at least a few who were listening that day in the temple were there twenty-one years later to watch not a meek child, but an angry young man rage against the greed and hypocrisy He had first seen there as a boy.

I've always imagined an elderly rabbi who was just curious enough to stay for a while and listen to the young Jesus. Convicted by His words, the teacher does not stay for long. However, later that night he realizes the voice of God was indeed speaking through that most unlikely Galilean boy. Early the next morning he runs back to the temple to look for Jesus, only to find that His parents have already come and taken Him home.

I suppose the old rabbi of my imagination is really me. I would no doubt have been the one who would have stood in the back of the crowd and listened only as long as my busy schedule would have allowed. I would have made an immediate judgment on the boy: "He's too young. What does He know?" His poor circumstances would have made me certain that He had nothing of value to say. Yes, I'm certain that old man in my mind is me. But even as the rabbi in the song heard the voice of God, I trust that the Lord would have broken through the wall of my foolishness, as He does today. And though I'll never know for sure, I pray that I, too, would have come running back to find that little boy who spoke the words of God.

THE BAPTISM

In the desert a voice is crying,
"Prepare the way for Messiah's coming!"
A stone that makes men stumble
And a rock that makes them fall.

By the banks of the Jordan he was waiting
For the sign of the One who would surely come.
When he heard what the thunder now was saying,
It was clear this must be the Chosen One.

The deaf will hear and the dumb will talk.
The blind will see and the lame will walk.
A stone that makes men stumble
And a rock that makes them fall.

He came gently and stepped down into the water,
With the light of the Father in His face.
Son of God He had been since the beginning.
Now as Son of Man Jesus took His place.

Some denominations sprinkle; others immerse; each say their form better represents the true meaning of baptism. The dissension, I believe, is an indication of the fact that baptism is really a mystery. Who can say what the form "means"? We submit to baptism out of obedience to Jesus' command. Beyond that there's not much more to say. Having said that let me say a little bit more.

Baptism is literally a washing. It is symbolically a death, burial, and resurrection. It initiates the believer into a covenant and usually into a body of believers, so in that sense it may be seen to speak of a kind of new birth (. . . he who "is born of water.")[1] Submitting to baptism is a sign of a repentant heart. For such a simple act it can be seen to have many meanings.

The earliest teaching on baptism we have from the first century says that if no water can be found then one should simply use sand. The church fathers were obviously not as hung up on form as we are today. Perhaps they desired to be obedient to Christ more than to seem "correct." They weren't caught up in arguing about the form because they recognized something we have forgotten amidst our debate and that is that baptism is truly a mystery.

Jesus' baptism presents an even greater mystery. John the Baptist, who administered it, seemed to have had no idea what was going on and tried to talk his way out of it. After all, there was nothing mysterious about the baptism he was offering there in the wilderness. It was a baptism of repentance, pure and simple.[2] It did not initiate you into any denomination, as the Jewish form of baptism did. It was a simple but graphic way of letting people know that they needed washing, a cleansing from their sin.

Then all at once, there He was. Jesus, the Lamb of God, asking John to baptize Him, to wash away His sins (of which John knew He had none). What could this possibly mean? It would have made perfect sense if Jesus had asked to baptize John. But that was not what Jesus wanted. And so the sinner symbolically washed away the "sins" of the Sinless One. And the two cousins acted out what perhaps even to both of them was a mystery.

At that moment the voice of God was heard. "This is My beloved Son," He said, "in whom I am well pleased." It's hard to believe that the Father was pleased by the fact that Jesus had simply gotten wet. It was His obedience that pleased God. Jesus did something which, we must all confess, seemed especially meaningless, and yet somehow the Father saw the deepest meaning in what He had done. He saw obedience. "My Son," God said to Himself and everyone else who had ears to hear.

Children are constantly being called upon to do things they don't understand. My mother said, "Wash up," but I knew I'd be dirty again in five minutes. My father said, "Mow the lawn," but why? It would just grow back by next week. My daughter is in pain with an infection and I

ask her to be still while a doctor painfully sticks a long needle into her flesh. Obedience can often seem meaningless.

Perhaps the point is that there really isn't a point at all. Did even Jesus see the point of letting a crazy prophet dunk Him in the cold waters of the Jordan? What if the Father had said, "Stand on Your head." Then we would be left to argue about what that means and whether you should bend your legs or use a pillow or not, and so the same churches would no doubt split off, grumbling and carrying their pillows with them.

God said, "Get in the water!" And without protesting the obvious, Jesus obeyed. "I am well pleased," He responded, "My Son." You can almost feel the absolutely pure pride. God said, "Drink this cup of suffering," and Jesus, who had openly confessed that He didn't want to do it, said, "Yet not as I will, but as you will." And from that same radical obedience—an obedience that submits even to what may seem senseless, that does not demand to see the meaning of it all—from that kind of obedience came the salvation of the world.

SCANDALON

The seers and the prophets had foretold it long ago,
That the long-"awaited One" would make men stumble.
But they were looking for a king to conquer and to kill.
Who'd have ever thought He'd be so meek and humble?

He will be the Truth that will offend them one and all.
A stone that makes men stumble and a rock that makes them fall.
And many will be broken so that He can make them whole.
And many will be crushed and lose their own soul.

Along the path of life there lies this stubborn Scandalon
And all who come this way must be offended.
To some He is a barrier, to others He's the way,
For all should know the scandal of believing.

He will be the Truth that will offend them one and all.
A stone that makes men stumble and a rock that makes them fall.
And many will be broken so that He can make them whole.
And many will be crushed and lose their own soul.

It seems today the Scandalon offends no one at all.
The image we present can be stepped over.
Could it be that we are like the others long ago?
Will we ever learn to listen and to stumble?

He will be the Truth that will offend them one and all.
A stone that makes men stumble and a rock that makes them fall.
And many will be broken so that He can make them whole.
And many will be crushed and lose their own soul.

A stumbling block. A scandal. Few of us ever think of Jesus in those terms, yet both the Old and New Testaments present Him that way. It all started with a prophecy in Isaiah, "He will be a stone that causes men to stumble and a rock that makes them fall."[1] Isaiah understood, perhaps better than any of the prophets, that when the Messiah would come He would be an offense, a scandal. That is why he said, in another place, that He would be despised and rejected, a Man of Sorrows and familiar with suffering.[2]

The scandal actually began before Jesus was born. A young woman became pregnant before the wedding. We can detect the sting of the offense later in Jesus' life when the mocking crowd says, "Isn't this Mary's son . . .?"[3] In Jesus' day children were identified as being their father's sons—unless there was no father.

Upon the occasion of the birth the scandal only got worse. The long-awaited Messiah born in a stable, not a palace; wrapped in rags, not in silk; asleep in a feeding trough, not an ivory crib.

The scandal fanned into flame when the ministry of Jesus began. Now everyone who came into contact with Jesus, it seems, stumbled because of Him. The priests, whom we might have expected to recognize and glory in the coming of Messiah, were offended by Him. Twice Jesus destroyed their temple marketplace. His ultimate offense to the priesthood, however, was the offering of Himself as a perfect sacrifice, complete and totally pleasing to God, an offering the priests had tried for centuries to offer.

Yet when we think of the offense of Jesus it is usually the Pharisees who come to mind. In my mind's eye I see the frightened disciples asking Jesus, who had just spoken of eating His flesh and drinking His blood, "Do you know that the Pharisees were offended when they heard this?"[4]

We might be tempted to wait for an apology or at least an explanation from Jesus, but we would have a long wait.

The heart of Pharisaism was known as the "oral law." When Moses came down from the mountain he gave the Ten Commandments to the priests. But what were he and God doing for the rest of those forty days and nights? The Pharisees believed that God was giving Moses the oral law, which he then entrusted to the elders, the Pharisees' spiritual ancestors, they said. Jesus had no patience for their oral tradition, which He referred to as "rules taught by men." Their tradition was circumventing God's Law, He said, and, therefore, He took advantage of every occasion to break their laws.

Both priests and Pharisees, as well as the other "religious" people of Jesus' day, were offended by the company that He kept. The outcasts of Jewish society, the "sinners," the "people of the land," as the Pharisees called them. Tax collectors, prostitutes, and lepers were frequently gathered around Jesus. His forgiving stance toward them was more than the "religious" people could bear. He went so far as to pronounce their forgiveness, something the scribes and Pharisees knew only God Himself had the authority to do.[5] And, of course, they were right.

Jesus' own disciples stumbled because of Him. In John 6 Jesus spoke of eating His flesh and drinking His blood. John tells us that upon hearing this many of His disciples were offended and left. "This is a hard teaching," they said. "Who can accept it?"[6] I wonder how many other "hard sayings" it had taken to bring them to this point. Once again, as they were leaving, you might have expected at least an explanation from Jesus, "No, you misunderstood. I know these things are hard to hear but just hang in there a little longer and it will all make sense."

Instead Jesus turned to the Twelve, who remained and said, "Are you going to leave as well?"

As usual, Peter spoke first. "To whom can we go?" he said.

Some imagine this as a great statement of faith, that in the face of the rejection of the others, Peter nonetheless remained faithful. I agree with Malcolm Muggeridge who called Peter's statement "loyal despair." That, I believe, is the tone of his response. "Yes, the scandal is hard to bear, and no, I don't understand why You seem to be driving followers away instead of doing what You can to attract them," Peter was saying. "But I also recognize that You, Jesus, have the words of eternal life and despite all the rest, there is nowhere else to go!"

The scandal forces us to make that kind of radical decision, which, on face value, can look pretty foolish. But there is nowhere else to go, and so we believe and we trust. And above all, we stay with Jesus.

If anyone should have been immune from stumbling because of Jesus it should have been John the Baptist. From the womb John knew who Jesus was, since his mother Elizabeth told Mary, The instant I heard your voice, my baby leaped for joy.[7] John recognized, it seems, even the embryonic Jesus! It is John who first speaks of the dignity of Jesus and exclaims, "Behold! The Lamb of God!"[8] It is he who hears the very voice of God say, "This is My beloved Son . . ." when John baptizes Jesus. The Baptist should have known better.

In Matthew 11 John succumbs to the scandal of Jesus. John is in prison, not for doing something wrong but for doing something right: publicly denouncing the adulterous relationship Herod was having with his brother's wife. For that John ended up in the dungeon. From prison he heard that Jesus had gone back to Galilee to preach and teach. We can only assume that he expected Jesus to come and get him out of prison, by whatever means. The Baptist be-

lieves himself to have been deserted by his close friend and relative.

In his despair, John sent some of his disciples to Jesus with a staggering question. "Are You the one who was to come, or should we expect someone else?" It is the most startling question in the New Testament. It reveals that even John has stumbled because of Him. "Blessed is the man who does not stumble because of Me," is the reply Jesus sends back. The word used for stumble is a verbal form of the noun *scandalon*. The verse could be translated, "Blessed is the man who is not scandalized by Me."

The heart of our offense with Jesus is that He fails to meet our expectations. The priests and Pharisees expected a different sort of Messiah. It never occurred to John the Baptist that he would end up in prison. That, I believe, is the heart of the scandal. If it is truly Jesus Himself you are getting close to, He will fail to meet your expectations sooner or later and you will stumble, like all the rest.

Everyone who comes to know Jesus stumbles because of Him. He fails to meet our wrong expectations. He calls us to do impossible things or to become something we think we could never become. This is His way of teaching us how much we need Him. He breaks us to pieces so that He can put us back together in His image.

(Another Jesus is preached in America. He is different altogether. He never does anything unexpected. He is safe and predictable and easy to follow. He answers every prayer that is formulated correctly and accompanied by the right "love gift." He is easily "stepped over." That is not the Jesus of the Bible. The last thing He is, is safe.)

In the face of failed expectations often all we can do is respond as Peter did in the face of the SCANDALON: "Where else can we go? You alone have the words of eternal life." True faith is born at precisely that point.

THE LAMB IS A LION

Weak from the journey,
The long traveling days.
Hungry to worship,
To join in the praise.
Shock met with anger
That burned on His face,
As He entered the wasteland
Of that barren place.

And the Lamb is a Lion
Who's roaring with rage
At the empty religion
That's filling their days.
They'll flee from the harm
Of the Carpenter's strong arm,
And come to know the scourging
Anger of the Lord.

The priests and the merchants
Demanded some proof.
For their hearts were hardened
And blind to the truth.
That Satan's own law
Is to sell and to buy.
But God's only Way
Is to give and to die.

And the Lamb is a Lion
Who's roaring with rage
At the empty religion
That's filling their days.
They'll flee from the harm
Of the Carpenter's strong arm,

And come to know the scourging
Anger of the Lord.

The noise and confusion gave way to His word.
At last sacred silence so God could be heard.

And the Lamb is a Lion
Who's roaring with rage
At the empty religion
That's filling their days.
They'll flee from the harm
Of the Carpenter's strong arm,
And come to know the scourging
Anger of the Lord.

I go to the Christian conventions and see the long lines of displays: Jesus soap, Jesus T-shirts, Christian Trivial Pursuit, the endless collections of records and tapes. I wonder sometimes, does Jesus want someone to turn all these tables over as He did in the temple bazaar? Might He even want *me* to turn them over, right now, this very minute? But then I realize that I might destroy some of my own product. And wouldn't it be a useless gesture anyway?

If someone else were to turn my own tables over, I think I would applaud. I wouldn't try to stop them. In fact, no one tried to stop Jesus when He wrecked the market that had been set up in the Gentile's place of prayer. Most of the people seemed to approve, even the Pharisees. Nobody asked Jesus why He did such a thing. All they wondered was, *Who has given Him the authority?*

The word is *commercialism*. That's how most people see the temple expulsion: Jesus' fight against the merchants

who were turning His Father's house into a marketplace, a "den of robbers." There was a considerable mark-up on the merchandise inside the temple. A dove, the sacrifice of the poor, which cost a few pennies outside the temple, could cost as much as seventy inside. That is why we hear Jesus specifically address the "sellers of doves." He was indignant that the poor were being ripped off. And that is a large part of the lesson. But there is more.

(First, let's remember that the temple expulsion happened twice. In the gospel of John, the first public thing Jesus did was clear the traders from the temple. His disciples remembered a psalm that said, "Zeal for your house will consume me."[1] In the synoptic gospels we read of the second expulsion. It took place during the last week of His ministry and was one of the last public things He did. Here Jesus made the same commotion but quoted Isaiah and Jeremiah to justify his actions. Biblical scholars who promote the idea that John has simply misplaced the temple expulsion in his narrative overlook the far simpler solution: It happened twice. Once, as the first public act of Jesus. Then again, as perhaps the last.)

As much as being upset about the commerciality of the whole business, Jesus was angered at the disregard that was being shown the Gentiles. The merchants had set up their booths in the Court of the Gentiles, a place reserved for prayer for non-Jewish believers, commonly referred to as "God-fearers," of whom there were many. It was a courtyard surrounded by a low wall, separating it from the inner courts, which were reserved for Jews only. If Gentiles ventured any closer to the temple complex, guards were under strict orders to put them to death. The court where the merchants had set up shop was the only place for Gentiles to offer prayers of thanksgiving and praise to their God (whom they were acknowledging as being the one true God by their very presence in the temple). Now, with the

clamor of the merchants going on all around, they had no place to be alone with the Lord.

"My house will be called a house of prayer . . ." Jesus thunders back at the merchants. Now we understand that He was as upset about the Gentiles not having a place to pray as He was with the commercialism of the merchants.

As I walk up and down, looking at all the Christian paraphernalia, I promise I will go on listening for that gentle Voice to say, "All right, now's the time! Wreck the place!" And when I hear it, God give me the courage to obey, even if my own "product" gets destroyed in the process.

In the meantime I'll also listen for that Voice that constantly bids me to pray, to speak of my frustrations and failures, of my hopes and fears. "Open wide your heart and tell Me of your love and your longing to love Me more," Jesus says. That same voice also says, "Make a place for those who also long to speak to Me. Do absolutely nothing to hinder them and absolutely everything to help them. Even if you must turn over a few tables in the process."

THE NAZARENE

The Nazarene had come to live the life of every man.
And He felt the fascination of the stars.
And as He wandered through this weary world,
He wondered and He wept,
For there were so few who'd listen to His call.

He came, He saw, He surrendered all,
So that we might be born again.
And the fact of His humanity was there for all to see.
For He was unlike any other man
And yet so much like me.

The Nazarene could hunger and the Nazarene could cry,
And He could laugh with all the fullness of His heart.
And those who hardly knew Him,
And those who knew Him well,
Could feel the contradiction from the start.

He came, He saw, He surrendered all,
So that we might be born again.
And the fact of His humanity was there for all to see.
For He was unlike any other man
And yet so much like me.

Anyone who has suffered through high school Latin is familiar with the phrase, *"Veni, vidi, vici."* It means, "I came, I saw, I conquered." It is found in a letter Julius Caesar wrote to Amautius describing his victory at Zela in 47 B.C. It was Caesar's motto.

But his empire finally crumbled, and he who was the conqueror became the conquered.

Jesus, who possessed infinitely greater power, lived His life by a strange and unexpected twist of Caesar's saying. Jesus lived by the motto, "I came, I saw, I surrendered." By living out this unorthodox pronouncement Jesus demonstrated that what the world regards as power is really impotence. True victory is only possible through surrender.

Jesus' primary surrender was to the taking on of human flesh, the Incarnation. It was this surrender that made possible the cross. Although He might have grasped equality with God, He nonetheless surrendered to becoming human out of obedience to the Father.[1] And so His human life began as it would end, based on the paradox of victory through surrender.

Jesus' total embrace of humanity, His becoming like us, is the basis of our hope to someday be like Him. His identification with our frailty provides our confidence that someday we will cast aside our fragile, fallen humanity and see Him as He is.[2]

So we are caught up in a dilemma. We follow a Savior who conquers by allowing Himself to be conquered, who saves us by not allowing Himself to be saved. He bids us follow in the same way. The fact of His humanity is our hope for salvation.

THE GENTLE HEALER

The Gentle Healer came into our town today.
He touched blind eyes and their darkness left to stay.
But more than the blindness, He took their sins away.
The Gentle Healer came into our town today.

The Gentle Healer came into our town today.
He spoke one word that was all He had to say.
And the one who had died just rose up straight away.
The Gentle Healer came into our town today.

Oh, He seems like just an ordinary man.
With dirty feet and rough but gentle hands.
But the words He says are hard to understand.
And yet He seems like just an ordinary man.

The Gentle Healer, He left our town today.
I just looked around and found He'd gone away.
Some folks from town who've followed Him, they say,
That the Gentle Healer is the Truth, the Life, the Way.

When we read the Gospels we sometimes lose sight of the ordinary people whose lives were impacted when they met Jesus. This is a fictional story based on a fictional song. . . .

Who would have ever believed that someone like Him would come to a sleepy little town like Bethsaida? Don't misunderstand me, I love my town and the hills and the Sea of Tiberias. It has always been my home. And always will be, I hope.

My father gave his name to me, Joshub, though that is not what I am called by most in town. "Slow one," they call out across the street, "Raca," or "Stupid!" I don't really mind. The Creator, blessed be He, must have wanted me this way. And I think I must still be a happier man than most.

Since my parents' death I make my living by helping out around the village. The carpenter, Nathan, lets me clean out his shop sometimes and sleep there when the weather's bad. The fishermen allow me to help them with their nets and sometimes give me of their catch to eat.

That is how I met Phillip, one of the followers of the Rabbi from Nazareth. He was a fisherman, basically a kind man, although not one you would expect to find following a religious teacher. Like the other fishermen, he could be rough in his talk and his ways. Although, once he did rebuke some of the others for speaking cruelly to me, though I never thanked him for it. When he left to follow Jesus I rarely saw him in town, except when the Teacher Himself would come.

The first time I ever saw Jesus I was rounding the corner on my way into Nathan's shop and almost knocked the Rabbi down. He was leaning in the doorway, watching Nathan at work on a plow handle and giving him advice

on how to better shape the wood. I suppose it was my own clumsy fault.

He looked at me not with anger or surprise but with a sort of gentle familiarity, as if He knew me. My father used to look at me like that when the boys would make me cry with their taunts.

"Forgive me, Rabbi," I said.

"You are Joshub," said He.

"Yes, Master," I replied, "though I am called by other names in this town."

"I understand," Jesus said kindly, "some call Me by other names as well."

He would have continued talking with me but I broke away out of embarrassment. Later I thought the better of it and went back, hoping to see Him. But He and His disciples had already left.

The next time I saw Him was many months later. I must confess He had not entered my mind since that day at the carpenter's shop. The fishing had been slow for days, so I knew there would be no work for me at the shore. And also no food. It was a beautiful sunny day and since the village seemed to be deserted I went up into the mountains to wander alone, to look out over the sea, and to be by myself with no one to make fun of me.

As I approached the top of a small ridge I heard the murmuring of a crowd. I topped the hill and saw the next valley filled with people. There were thousands! They covered the hillside, men, women, and children all sitting and straining to hear someone who was speaking from the middle of the throng. Although I could not get close enough to see, I knew it must be Him, Jesus.

I pressed in as close as I could and tried my best to listen. Though I could make out His words, words never meant all that much to me. I am so dull. And besides by

this time my stomach was churning, aching of emptiness. Just as I was dozing off I heard a barocha being pronounced for the meal. Needless to say this roused me quickly.

"Blessed be Thou, Eternal Creator of the Universe, who makes bread come forth from the earth."

It was the Teacher, giving the blessing over a handful of fish and bread. I thought to myself that He and His disciples were about to have their noon meal. But there was hardly enough food there, even for them.

He placed the fish and bread into some baskets the disciples were holding and to everyone's amazement, told them to give the crowd something to eat. *What a nice but hopeless gesture*, I thought to myself, *perhaps this will cause the others to share*.

A group close by, some of the same men who used to taunt me as a boy, now taunted Jesus for this foolishness.

"Yes," they mocked, "we would all like our lunch baskets filled, if you please."

It was my old acquaintance, Phillip, who obliged them. "Give me your baskets," he said, and proceeded to scoop them full of food.

The men, for once, were speechless.

Those who were close to Jesus knew at once of the miracle. The ones at the back of the crowd only thought some wealthy person had generously provided food. But there were no wealthy people there that day.

I ate my fill and laid back on the green grass, listening to the voice of the Rabbi. It was an ordinary voice, but full of kindness. It lulled me to sleep. When I awoke everyone, including the Teacher, was gone.

It was a year or more before I saw Him again. It was the last time. He had been much on my mind since that day in the mountains, when all that great crowd was fed. Since then, every time I broke bread I thought of Him and that

day and the sunshine. When I helped the fishermen take
their catch from the nets I remembered Jesus, who needed
no nets, calm and smiling in the midst of the hungry crowd.
I tried to remember His words of that day, but all I could
recall was Him and what He had done. What He did
meant more than words.

It was a cool spring evening. I remember the season
because Passover was near. He came quietly into town, no
one was even aware of His presence here. I only knew because I saw Phillip coming from his father's house. From
that I understood that the Teacher must be in town.

Phillip greeted me with great kindness. He remembered
my name and asked how I was faring and if the men still
made fun of me and my slowness. He had changed over
the years since I had known him. He was now more like
the Rabbi he followed. Yet he was nervous and kept looking over his shoulder into the shadows as if he expected to
find someone lurking there.

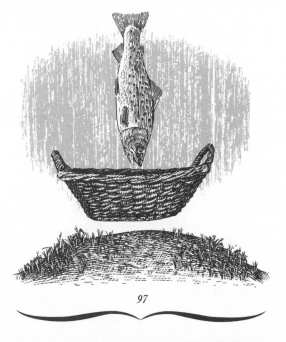

I don't remember what I said to him. I only asked where the Rabbi was staying. He told me it was to be kept a secret but he knew I could be trusted. The Rabbi was staying at Nathan's shop for the night. I thought it strange that He should be staying there and not in Nathan's home, as was His custom. But I asked no questions as Phillip was already heading off into the night in that direction.

I followed Phillip to the place. He entered with a whisper at the door. In the dim light of a single candle I saw only Jesus and His disciples. They looked surprised to see me, a stranger, all of a sudden in their midst.

"It is all right," Phillip said to calm them. "This is Joshub, he is a friend."

Jesus sat in the corner with His back resting against the cool stone wall. He looked so tired. In His hands was one of Nathan's mallets. He kept shifting it from one hand to the other.

Jesus looked up at me and with a weary smile said, "I know you."

"Yes, Rabbi," I said nervously, "I almost knocked you down once, but that was long ago."

"They call you names," he said, "stupid and slow, a fool." As He spoke those words I could see on His face the pain hearing them all these years had caused me.

"But you're not stupid, Joshub," Jesus gently said, "within your grasp this very night is all the Wisdom of God." With that He dropped the mallet and grasped my hand.

"Never let them call you slow, Joshub. Wisdom is yours. Truth. Do you believe this?" He asked.

"Lord," said I, "I am not a man of words. What does wisdom have to do with a fool like me?"

A tear ran down Jesus' face. "You are wiser than you know." With that He rested Himself against the wall. His voice was darker as He spoke, "This might be the last time

we see each other, My friend. I'm on My way to Jerusalem."

When I heard Jesus call me "friend" something moved inside me. I realized that of all the names I had been called, no one had ever called me by that name.

"I would like to see you again, Jesus, ... my friend," I stuttered, embarrassed at my words. I thought of running out that very moment.

"Is that really what you want?" Jesus said.

"That is all I desire, Lord."

"Then you shall have all you desire."

The next morning I awoke to Nathan, the carpenter, trying to rouse me. Jesus and His disciples were gone.

"Joshub, what are you doing?" he asked. "What is that in your hand?"

I looked and there in my hand was the carpenter's mallet Jesus had been holding the night before.

(Joshub became the leader of the small Christian community in Bethsaida. In later years he was revered for his understanding and kindness. He was buried on a hillside outside Bethsaida, overlooking the sea, with a carpenter's mallet in his hand.)

THE WEDDING

Lord of Light,
Please come to this wedding.
Take the doubt and darkness away.
Turn the water of lifeless living
To the wine of gladness, we pray.

Mother Mary's gently requesting,
That You might do whatever You can.
Though she may be impatient,
She loves You.
And so she asks what she can't understand.

Lord of Light,
Please come to this wedding.
Take the doubt and darkness away.
Turn the water of lifeless living
To the wine of gladness, we pray.

So amidst the laughter and feasting,
There sits Jesus, full with the fun!
He has made them wine
Because He is longing
For a wedding that's yet to come.

Lord of Light,
Please come to this wedding.
Take the doubt and darkness away.
Turn the water of lifeless living
To the wine of gladness, we pray.

My grandmother was known as perhaps the best Bible teacher in Knoxville. That didn't bother my grandfather even though he was the pastor of the largest church in the city. In his time women weren't supposed to outshine their husbands in anything. Yet he didn't seem to mind. I grew up hearing stories of lumbering University of Tennessee (U.T.) football players hobbling to her Sunday morning class on crutches to hear this petite and powerful teacher.

I came to know her much later in life as a fragile little form, lying in a bed in a nursing home. She would always ask me to read the Bible to her on those visits and would correct any omissions or incorrect pronunciations I would make. Later on, after her tired mind had let go of her name and who she was, and who I was, she could still tell if anyone who read to her had missed a word, from Genesis to Revelation.

She died when I was seventeen. The funeral home was packed with family members and friends, everyone talking and remembering stories about her and my grandfather. What was supposed to be a wake quickly turned into a party that grew so loud two employees of the funeral home had to finally come in and ask us to quiet down out of respect to the other clients. I don't remember anyone using the obvious "wake the dead" line. (If no one did, they missed a wonderful opportunity!)

I've often heard preachers say at funerals that it is really a celebration, but they usually aren't very convincing, least of all to those closest to the deceased. Yet this was a celebration. It was an outright party! Had it gone on the police would have no doubt been called in to arrest us for disturbing the peace. (Most of us felt as if the peace of that place needed some disturbing.)

Wherever and whenever Christians come together, parties should break out because we follow a Savior who is

preoccupied with them. Whenever Jesus wasn't preaching or teaching you'd find Him at a party. It might be at a tax collector's or at a Pharisee's home. The guests might include powerful men in the community or the riffraff. What seemed to bother the stuffy, "religious" types wasn't that Jesus went to parties, but that He seemed to enjoy Himself too much. That, I believe, is why they called Him a glutton and winebibber.

It was at just such a party that Jesus performed His first miracle. The occasion was a wedding banquet. Tradition tells us it was the disciple John's wedding and that makes sense, since Mary (who was the cousin of John's mother) seems to feel some sort of responsibility to the guests and since John has inside knowledge of events that took place at the party, which no one else seems to be aware of. The miracle was the turning of the water into wine, some four hundred gallons of it!

I've heard many good theological explanations about that first miracle. "Jesus simply speeded up a natural process because, of course, in nature grapevines take water and turn them into wine," some say. "All miracles are really just nature speeded up." Such explanations miss the point, I think. The point is that running out of wine is the surest way of bringing a party to a grinding halt, and Jesus' provision allowed the party to go on.

The concept of the party was important not only to Jesus but to the early church as well. The fellowship of the early Christians was a primary source of evangelism in those first days of the faith. They enjoyed the favor of all the people as the pagans witnessed the joy of their gatherings.[1] "They have had too much wine," some onlookers said at Pentecost.[2] Parties are almost as important as prayer for a Christian because, if you think about it, the climax of the history of this world takes place at a party.

It's called the "Marriage Supper of the Lamb" and if

what the Bible says is true, it will quite literally be the party of all time. As far back as Isaiah the prophets were catching glimpses of it. God will prepare "a banquet of aged wine."³ You can almost hear the prophet's mouth watering.

If Jesus seemed to be particularly excited about the wedding feast that day in Cana, I believe it was because He was looking ahead to that final feast, where He, the Bridegroom will finally be brought together with us, His Bride. And if He gave in to His mother's request about the wine at that wedding banquet, it was because He was longing for a taste of that "aged wine" Isaiah promised to Him and to us at a party where no one would dream of coming in and telling us to quiet down.

FORGIVING EYES

Surrounded with shouts, the cruel accusations,
Dragged to the court, no hope of salvation,
All hope was lost for those who had caught me
Knew who I was, they knew all about me.

I thought it seemed strange as we entered in,
They stopped a young Rabbi to ask His opinion.
Caught in the act, their reason for hating,
My body could feel the stones that were waiting.

My judge, a man from Galilee,
In His eyes so gentle I could see
A Father and a Brother and a Son.

Just as I saw Him the hope I had lost became born again.
I was not hopeless.
Though I'd been lost, now I felt I was found
When He looked at me
With His forgiving eyes.

The crowd gathered round so angry and violent.
But He stood beside me peaceful and silent.
Then with a word, with one question, He showed them
That they too were guilty and could not condemn.

The next thing I knew He asked me, "Where are they?"
When I looked around, the courtyard was empty.
The stones gathered 'round, the warm morning sunlight,
He'd made the darkness perfectly light.

In this new light now I understood,
He would not condemn me though He could.
For He would be condemned someday for me.

Just as I saw Him the hope I had lost became born again.
I was not hopeless.

Though I'd been lost, now I felt I was found
When He looked at me
With His forgiving eyes.

The story of the woman taken in adultery is unique in the New Testament. Some translations place a line before and after the passage to set it apart from the rest of the text. Others will footnote it with the statement: "The most reliable texts do not contain John 7:53— 8:11."

I remember the first time I was made aware of the problem with the text in one of my Bible classes at the university. As the professor commented on the textual problems I could feel my face getting hot. I wondered if this was the time for me to stand up and fight for the authority of the Bible. I lacked the courage to speak up and challenge him, but I did research the passage later on my own. I discovered that what he said was right. The passage doesn't appear in the oldest and most reliable Greek texts. When it does appear in the later ones, it is found in different places. In one ancient text it even appears in Luke! For this reason scholars refer to it as a "textual floater." The textual commentary that accompanies the United Bible Societies' Greek New Testament lists pages of problems with the textual authenticity of the passage, but low and behold, they include the passage in their Greek text of John, although at the end of the Gospel.

No one knows for sure just why this particular passage floats around and sometimes disappears the way it does. The explanation that makes the most sense to me proposes that the original manuscript of John did indeed contain the

story of the woman caught in adultery. As time went on, however, the disturbing story of Jesus forgiving the adulteress, without belaboring her sin, without really even condemning her, became more and more of an embarrassment to the church, so the scribes began to simply leave it out. Adultery was a big problem in the early church, as it is today.

Despite its textual problems and the fact that it seems to disrupt the chronology of chapter 8, the passage is its own best witness for its authenticity. Few believers, even the most scholarly, are able to say it does not represent a true occurrence from the life of Jesus. Standing on its own, the way it does, the story of the adulterous woman has always spoken to me in an extraordinarily powerful way. The many details John provides make it easy to imagine the setting and the story. . . .

It was just after dawn. A large crowd had gathered around Jesus in the temple court. Just as He was sitting down to teach, the Pharisees brought in a woman. It was a trap, a "set up," both for the woman and Jesus. Perhaps that's why, from the start, He seems to be on her side.

There is little doubt that she was guilty. The law required witnesses. That's why the Pharisees kept insisting she was caught "in the act." "Now, what do you say?" they asked Jesus. The trap was set and the woman was the bait.

You have to give the Pharisees credit. They knew how to construct a trap. Whichever way Jesus answered, He would be in real trouble. If He said, "Let her go," then He would not be upholding the law, which prescribed death for adultery. If He said, "Put her to death," He would be in trouble with the Romans, who ruled the Jews and had taken the power of capital punishment away from them.

Jesus seemed calm. Having stood up He now bent back down again and began to write with His finger in the dust. The word that's used to describe His action literally

means "to write down," so it's safe to say He wasn't doodling but actually writing something. Some speculate He was writing the names of people in the crowd who were also guilty of the same sin. Some think, because of a variant text, that He was making a list of their sins. We cannot tell from the text exactly what He was writing. Because of a passage in Jeremiah (17:13), I believe it was a list of names.

The Pharisees kept pushing Jesus for an answer. He stood up and calmly said, "If anyone of you is without sin, let him be the first to throw a stone at her!" He then resumed His position on the ground and began again to write in the dust.

The power of conviction caused everyone to leave, the older ones first, until only Jesus and the woman were left, alone in the courtyard. The dialogue that followed contained an almost medieval simplicity.

Jesus stood up and asked a gentle question. "Woman, where are they? Has no one condemned you?"

"No one, sir," she said.

"Then neither do I condemn you. Go now and leave your life of sin."

Yes, it is a disturbing story. No lecture. No condemnation. Only a word of kindness and a simple command to stop. If we didn't know better (because of Jesus' other words on the subject), we might think that He was indeed being "soft" on adultery. But we do know better. As Malcolm Muggeridge said, Jesus would not condemn the woman because He would be condemned for her. It is impossible for us to imagine the relief of the woman, having just been snatched from death. Most of us will not know such a sense of relief until we stand before our Judge on the last day and realize that He is also our Savior.

But what about the other person who sinned with the woman? Someone will always bring up the subject of the

man who had committed adultery with her. Was he one of the Pharisees? Is that why he was allowed to escape? After all, that particular sin requires two people.

There is a good reason for his not appearing. He is you and me! We are, every one of us, as guilty as the man who got away. We think we have escaped, when, in fact, we are as good as dead unless we find our own way to that One, sitting alone in the temple court, with stones scattered at His feet, writing thoughtfully with His finger in the sand.

WHAT WILL IT TAKE

What will it take to keep you from Jesus?
Keep you from heeding His call?
The simple excuse of a heart that is hard,
A reason that's nothing at all.

There was a man who was known by his money.
He was as rich as could be.
But deep in his heart was a voice that was crying,
Telling him he wasn't free.
When he questioned the Master concerning his problem,
The answer took his breath away.
For his money had come to mean more than his soul
And forever would stand in his way.

What will it take to keep you from Jesus?
Keep you from heeding His call?
The simple excuse of a heart that is hard,
A reason that's nothing at all.

How long before you stop with your reasons?
And take your defenses away?
It's only a lie that keeps you from following.
Don't let it stand in your way.

So many excuses and so many lies
Are blocking the Light and the Way.
But the final decision to follow the Lord
Can shatter and blow them away.

Once there was one who was lame in his body,
Sick in his body and soul.
Though he didn't know all the facts about Jesus
He knew that he longed to be whole.
So with some of his friends he went seeking and found Him,
But so many stood in their way.

So they tore through the roof and they lowered him down
For nothing could keep him away.

What will it take to keep you from Jesus?
Keep you from heeding His call?
The simple excuse of a heart that is hard,
A reason that's nothing at all.

Ask people who don't believe in Jesus what is keeping them from making a decision to follow Him, and most of the time they'll give you a reason. It's not that they don't know why. They usually do.

Sometimes the reasons are weighty: A loved one died needlessly and they were never able to get over it. Or they suffered for no apparent reason. In the face of those kinds of hurting people, we who know Christ must be faithful to pray for them and to reflect the gentleness and patience of Jesus.

Often, however, the reasons aren't so weighty: They heard someone say that they heard somebody else say that they heard a rumor that a local preacher was accused of having an affair. Or once, a long time ago, they found a church service boring and decided then and there never to go back. These people need to have their excuses challenged in love and be shown that Christ Himself desires that nothing should stand between them and His love.

Many Christians' lives are a testimony to the fact that they would allow nothing to keep them away from Jesus. The list is endless: the hardened criminal who reached out and found Christ waiting there to save him; the ones who despite intense pain or deformity (or perhaps because of them) found Jesus to be all they could ever need or want.

Two examples come to mind from the Gospels: a man who allowed a simple excuse to keep him away from Jesus and another, a man who would let nothing hold him back.

The first is the story of the rich young ruler.[1] At first glance it seems that the young man was truly desirous of finding eternal life. He hounds Jesus with questions, pushing for specifics. Jesus' answers are short and to the point and, for once at least, were what someone might expect from a religious teacher.

"Obey the commands," Jesus tells the persistent man.

"Which ones?" he responds.

After a brief recital of six of the most basic commandments, the young man presses further, "All these I have kept, what do I still lack?"

The rich young ruler's claim to have kept the commandments causes Jesus to make a statement that reveals the fact that the pious youngster had, in fact, broken the very first one. Jesus asks him to sell all his possessions and give the money to the poor. That, He says, is the way to have true treasure.

The rich young ruler makes no response. Matthew simply says he "went away sad, because he had great wealth."[2] Jesus' demand reveals that he had not kept all the commandments, as he had self-righteously claimed before. His inability to let go of his money was the surest indication that he had made money his god, and thereby violated the very first commandment.

(An ancient tradition says the rich young ruler later changed his mind, sold his possessions, and became a follower of Jesus. We can only hope it is true.)

The other example that comes to mind is the paralytic man whose friends had to carry him to Jesus.[3] Mark tells us that Jesus had just returned to Capernaum. Matthew calls it "his own town,"[4] which leads us to think that Jesus settled in Capernaum after His expulsion from Nazareth. A

large crowd was present to hear Him speak; so many, in fact, that the paralytic and his friends couldn't even get to the door of the house where Jesus was teaching. So the paralytic's friends climbed up on the roof, dismantled the tiles, and lowered the man into the house. Picture, if you can, the lesson being interrupted by someone being lowered in from the ceiling! I can imagine a smile of amusement on Jesus' face at the sight of such faith. The man would allow nothing to keep him from Jesus, not the roof, which was broken through, not his paralysis, or even the fear of the crowd! In response to his faith, Jesus forgave his sins and healed him of the paralysis. He walked home with great joy, in contrast to the rich man who went away sad.

What is keeping you and me from Jesus? Chances are we know exactly what it is: some material desire, like a new house or car; some hurt we refuse to forgive; some sin that needs to be confessed and forgiven. We can stubbornly hold on, like the rich man, and spend the rest of our lives "going away sad." Or we can make that final decision: Nothing will stand between us and Jesus. We might have to ask some friends to carry us to find the help we need to find Him—a church, or perhaps a rehab center. We must ask for the faith to be healed of whatever it is that's paralyzing us. Make the decision now that nothing will separate you from His love whether it is something as flimsy as a dollar bill or as hard as a tile roof.

LONELINESS

When they told you of the Baptist,
Of what Herod's men had done,
You had to flee into the wilderness
To try to ease Your mind,
And just to be alone.
And I'm certain that You'll meet me there today.

'Cause You walked in lonely places.
You felt the empty spaces
That living in a lonely world can cause.
And knowing that You're with me now,
And knowing that You care somehow,
Makes my loneliness just draw me close to You.

In Gethsemane You needed someone to be near,
And so You called on Peter, James, and John,
Just to have somebody close to You,
Even if they were asleep,
Even though they never seemed to understand.

That You walk in lonely places.
You fill the empty spaces
That living in a lonely world can cause.
And knowing that You're with me now,
And knowing that You care somehow,
Makes my loneliness just draw me close to You.

I have always struggled with loneliness. It's not because I don't have a wonderful family and friends. Sometimes it's precisely because they are so special and so numerous that I feel that way. Unless you suffer from the same feeling, you'll probably think that's a bit crazy. Someone once described such loneliness as being ill at ease with the world but at peace with the universe. There is no apparent reason, but feelings don't need reasons.

At those lonely times I often think about Jesus. It's no surprise that all four Gospels talk about His loneliness and preference for "lonely places." You can sense it between the lines of many of those passages, a holy melancholy. A lonely Messiah.

In the midst of His own disciples, whom He loved with so much tenderness, Jesus is so often misunderstood. They question. They doubt. They constantly miss whatever point He is trying to make.

When Jesus' family, believing Him to be out of His mind, come to take charge of Him, His response has a dull and lonely sound, "Who are My mother and my brothers?"[1] When the crowd tries to force Him to become their "bread king," Jesus flees to the wilderness.[2] I can almost see Him wandering about there, talking to Himself and His Father, the only One who really understood.

John the Baptist, Jesus' cousin and friend, is senselessly murdered, and Jesus' response is to retreat, by Himself.[3] Luke tells us that He often withdrew to "lonely places."[4]

When Jesus felt alone, it was because His Father was so visibly absent in the world. Jesus sought His presence in lonely places. I wonder if their hearts resonated together with loneliness . . . for each other.

We all know what it's like to be misunderstood by those we love the most, to feel as if we are the only ones in the world going through what we're going through, the feeling

that life is meaningless. Yet in Christ everything has meaning. There is no darkness in Him, for He is Light. So where does loneliness fit in? The Gospels tell us that when Jesus retreated to those lonely places it was for prayer. In that, we can see a purpose in loneliness, both for Jesus and for us. That sense of "aloneness" forced Jesus to flee to a lonely place, to pray, to pour out His heart to the Father. One great conclusion is at the heart of Jesus' remedy for loneliness: If God, the Father of Jesus, really does exist, then none of us are alone, and indeed can never be.

(If God is merely a cold and impersonal God, we would be more lonely still. As we tend to feel most alone in a crowd, wouldn't it be even more lonely in the presence of an all-powerful Being who simply didn't care?)

Every time we let loneliness take over our feelings, we have lost sight of that personal, caring, and loving Father. He is "Abba," our Papa. Even if no other person understands or cares, He does. That is the God Jesus fled to when He felt lonely. The same caring Father is there for us.

The humanity of Jesus might have caused Him to fear that He was alone. Our own flesh often speaks to us the same terrible message. Yet the voice of our Abba says, "Never will I leave you. Never will I forsake you. You are the apple of my eye, my chosen one, my beloved. How could you ever be lonely when I am here?"

THE THINGS WE LEAVE BEHIND

There sits Simon, foolish and wise.
Proudly he's tending his nets.
Jesus calls and the boats drift away.
And all that he owns he forgets.
But more than the nets he abandoned that day,
He found that his pride was soon fading away.
It's hard to imagine the freedom we find
From the things we leave behind.

The sightless beggar, pleading each day,
Catching the coins in his robe.
At finding Jesus he threw it away
And joyfully followed his Lord.
But more than the robe that he left by the way,
The darkness that dwelt in his heart went away.
It's hard to imagine the freedom we find
From the things we leave behind.

Matthew was mindful of taking the tax
And pressing the people to pay.
At hearing the call he responded in faith
And followed the Light and the Way.
And leaving the people so puzzled he found
That the greed in his heart was no longer around.
It's hard to imagine the freedom we find
From the things we leave behind.

I am not a prophet, nor the son of a prophet, but I do have one vision that reoccurs: I see a path disappearing in the distance. Either side is strewn with various objects. A cloak. A cane. An expensive car, the door left open, the keys still in the ignition. The list is endless. The objects represent things people have left to follow Jesus. In the vision I keep looking for things I have left behind for His sake.

Almost everyone who follows Jesus in the New Testament leaves something behind for His sake. Simon and the other disciples who were fishermen left their nets and boats. James and John, the sons of Zebedee, left their father in the process as well as a prosperous family business.[1] Archaeologists tell us they have uncovered a fish market, a "branch office" in Jerusalem that belonged to Zebedee (perhaps the first store in a chain called, "Captain Zee's?").

Matthew left behind an even more lucrative business, tax gathering. Not only do I see his tax booth abandoned alongside my visionary path, I see a pile of money on it. Once Matthew left his wealth to follow Jesus we never hear him mention money or power again! (Though the other disciples talk about it frequently.)

Others left things behind after they encountered Jesus. The blind beggar, who used his cloak to gather the coins he begged, jumped up and left the cloak lying there after Jesus gave him his sight.[2] The woman at the well ran off and forgot her water jar once she was confronted by this man who told her "everything she had ever done."[3] The woman who suffered from continual bleeding left a long line of doctors behind.[4] The son of the widow of Nain left an empty coffin lying there by the city gate.[5] The sinful woman left behind an empty alabaster perfume jar.[6] Lazarus, perhaps most miraculous of all, left behind a pile of grave clothes and an empty tomb.[7]

You can go on and on. The farther down the path you

get, the higher the possessions piled on either side. With each object the travelers left behind, and leave behind, a small piece of themselves, because a possession isn't a little something you own, as much as something that owns a little bit of you. We leave behind a part of our old self, our "old man." In return for whatever small thing we discard Jesus gives us a part of Himself in exchange. With Him is great freedom from those things we leave behind, freedom from that greatest self-possessing possession, our "self."[8]

DISTRESSING DISGUISE

He is in the pain. He is in the need.
He is in the poor, we are told to feed.
Though He was rich for us He became poor.
How could He give so much? What was it for?

In His distressing disguise
He waits for us to surmise
That we rob our brothers by all that we own,
And that's not the way He has shown.

Every time a faithful servant serves a brother that's in need,
What happens at that moment is a miracle indeed.
As they look to one another in an instant it is clear.
Only Jesus is visible for they've both disappeared.

He is in the hand that reaches out to give.
He is in the touch that causes us to live.
So speak with your life now as well as your tongue.
Shelter the homeless and care for the young.

In His distressing disguise
He hopes that we'll realize
That when we take care of the poorest of them
We've really done it to him.*

*Matthew 26:11.

If I were asked to articulate the one great desire that contains within it all my desires, I would answer simply that it is to see the face of Jesus.

A group from our church had been coming to the rescue mission on Tuesday nights. We would come in and set up all our musical "stuff." Someone would preach and lead singing. One night, I preached a sermon on "Jesus' Radical Identification With the Poor." It bombed in a big way, owing to the fact that the majority of the crowd was either in an alcoholic daze or hopelessly out of touch with reality, having just been "purged" from a local mental hospital. (That sermon would have been better spent on the rich and not the poor if it is worth repeating at all!)

A few weeks later as we were visiting the mission again, something miraculous happened to me. One of the brothers was spending time with an elderly man who bore all the classic signs of the "street alcoholic." My friend wasn't formally "ministering" to him as such, just spending time being with him. In a flash of "insight" the Lord spoke to me in a way I had never experienced. As I watched our team member open himself to this man, he disappeared and Christ became visible. And, as the alcoholic man received the lovingkindness of my friend, he, too, began to disappear and take on the image of Christ, who was present in his pain and need.

I am not saying Christ was living in this man simply because he was poor. Perhaps Jesus was present in the reaching out of both of them. I don't pretend to understand all that happened in that moment. Yet it was clear that the

two men were no longer visible. Paul would have said that both of them were hidden in Christ.

When Jesus came on the scene He announced that He had come to preach good news . . . to the poor. He proceeded to live a life of poverty, confessing on one occasion, "The Son of Man has no place to lay his head."[1] Whenever Jesus was asked about money He had to ask for some or obtain it in some miraculous way. For instance, when someone asked Him about paying taxes to Caesar, He had to ask someone to show Him a coin, precisely because He didn't have one Himself. On another occasion, when He and His disciples were pressed as to whether they were going to pay their temple tax, Jesus sent Peter to catch a fish, which had a coin inside.[2] Again the supposition is that He did not have a coin Himself, and so had to resort to extraordinary means to get one.

Jesus was penniless. Yet He instructed the rich young ruler to give away everything, knowing that his money was standing between him and total obedience to God. Jesus apparently asked the disciples to do the same thing, for at one point Peter responded, "Lord, we have left everything in order to follow you."[3] Jesus never tells us to do something He has not perfectly lived out. (He would never tell Peter to forgive seventy times unless it was clear in His own life that Jesus was prepared to forgive in such an extravagant way. He would never command our loving obedience to the Father unless it was first clear that He was perfect in His own love and obedience.)

So why would Jesus encourage people to give money to the poor when He never did so Himself? Isn't it simply because He had no money to give them? So what did Jesus give to the poor? The answer is, of course, He gave them Himself.

That is sometimes a difficult answer to hear for those of us who have decided to follow Jesus. That answer forces us

to see that it is not enough to give our money to the poor. Like Jesus, we must find a way to give ourselves, for in doing that, He is giving them Himself, through us.

THE STRANGER

You're still a stranger,
Wandering through the wilderness.
Still rejected, passed by on the street,
Starving, hungry, naked, and cold,
Pleading for a cup of cold water,
Dying all alone.

No longer mistaken
For the rebel You truly are.
You would still be tearing up temples,
Scattering the money of fools,
Scandalizing righteous pretenders,
Breaking all the rules.

No longer blinded.
In the light I see who You really are.
Never doing what is expected,
Far beyond the frame of my mind.
Caring for the poor and neglected,
Washing the feet of the beggar on the street,
While the rich men make believe You'll never come.

Jesus Christ, the Messiah, the Son of God, came to this world a stranger. (The apostle John said, "He was in the world, and though the world was made through Him, the world did not recognize Him. He came to that which was His own, but His own did not receive Him."[1])

Jesus, Himself, said, "I was a stranger and you invited me in."[2] In effect, He stated that not only had He come as a stranger but He had come for the stranger.

Jesus was estranged not because He wasn't what He should have been but rather because the world wasn't what it should be. Even though the world had been created through Him, it didn't recognize Him. The world suffered from the Fall as well as mankind. Even now it groans, the apostle Paul says.[3]

Yet certainly there were times when creation recognized the authority of Jesus. At least once He spoke to the winds. "Be quiet!" He said, in a way you or I might speak to our dog, and they obeyed. To the waves He said, "Calm down!" and they too obeyed. The disciples were terrified. "Who is this?" they stammered in fear. "Even the wind and the waves obey Him!"[4]

I sometimes ask myself if I might have felt safer that day in the water, rather than in the boat with someone who possessed such awesome power. When Jesus desired, He could lift the veil of His incarnation and speak in such a way that creation could recognize Him for who He was. Most often, however, He chose not to.

If the creation is groaning as Paul says, it is because you and I have had a hand in making it groan, and every day through our carelessness we continue to make it groan. In rare moments, I recognize the sound of creation's groaning, and realize we are all partially to blame.

My wife and I live in the country. We see a number of deer lying on the side of the road, especially in the fall.

When I see a dog or a cat hit on the side of the road the feeling I get is that it is a pity, but people's pets shouldn't be out on the road in the first place. But when I see a dead deer on the roadside, so graceful and so grotesque, the feeling I get is that it is the road that shouldn't have been there, nor the car that hit it, nor even my car. At times like that I sense creation's groaning and cannot help but groan a little myself.

God sometimes grants us the grace to groan along with creation. We, like the deer on the roadside, are forced to live in a world where most things are not as they should be. We groan because we too are estranged from our Creator. If given the chance, we would go on being estranged from Him. After all, it is not Jesus who is the real stranger, it is us. And one sad symptom of our estrangement is the sound of our groaning.

Though ultimately Jesus was not a stranger, He still did come for the stranger. If you invite the stranger in, Jesus says, it's as if you had invited Him. He has come so no one has to be a stranger ever again, including you and me (at least not strangers to each other and to Him).

After you've been a Christian for long enough, you discover a paradox: Once you become intimate with God you become even more a stranger to the world, for people in the world would have us groan all the more for knowing Him. If the creation did not recognize Jesus, then how much less can we expect it to recognize those who belong to Him, unless He gives us the grace, from time to time, to lift the veil of His incarnation in us and show the world His wonderful work of re-creation.

NATHANIEL

While walking down the road one day,
I saw the Savior coming my way.
He said in me there was no guile
So I thought I'd stop and talk awhile.

There was something different about Him.
You could see it in His eyes,
Warm and soft and wonderful,
And I knew He'd tell me no lies.

I said to Him, "How do You know me?
Do You know Phillip well?
He tells me You're the Son of God
And the King of Israel,
The King of Israel!"

There was something different about You.
You could see it in Your eyes,
Warm and soft and wonderful,
And I know You'll tell me no lies.

He said He'd seen me praying once,
Underneath an old fig tree.
I'd always gone there by myself.
No one ever prayed there with me.

I'd always gone to that tree to pray
To the God of Abraham.
If Jesus had heard the words I'd said,
Then He must be the Son of Man,
He must be the Son of Man.

There's something different about Him.
You can see it in His eyes,
Warm and soft and wonderful,

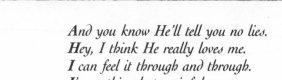

And you know He'll tell you no lies.
Hey, I think He really loves me.
I can feel it through and through.
I'm nothing but a sinful man,
But He's Jacob's dream come true.
*He's Jacob's dream come true.**

T his is one of the first songs I ever wrote. In the midst of reading some pretty boring material about the rabbis and their customs, I came upon a seemingly insignificant piece of information. The book I was studying said that the young rabbinic students made it a habit to study and pray outside, under trees, preferably fig trees, I suppose because of their symbolic association with Israel. By itself that seemed an almost meaningless piece of trivia until I remembered a detail from the Gospel of John.

In one of the more obscure passages of John's account, we read of a young man named Nathaniel (also known by the name Bartholomew). Jesus had already sought out and found Phillip, a friend of Nathaniel. Jesus had issued the call, "Follow me" to Phillip, who, without question, followed. Even as Andrew had first sought out Peter, now Phillip goes straight to Nathaniel with the good news that the Messiah has been found.

Nathaniel responds sarcastically, "Nazareth! Can anything good come from there?"—reflecting the attitude held by most Jews that nothing of any value could come from such a pagan place as Galilee.

Phillip, perhaps because he knows it's no use to argue

---

*John 1:43–51.

with someone as apparently pigheaded as Nathaniel, simply says, "Come and see."

As Nathaniel approaches Jesus, the Lord demonstrates His ability to know what is in a man's heart. (When Jesus first meets Peter He demonstrates that He already knows him inside out by giving him the nickname, "Cephas." In the midst of an argument Jesus could tell that someone was asking Him a question, not out of a sincere heart, but as a trap.) As Jesus sees Nathaniel approaching He says, "Here is a true Israelite, in whom there is no guile." Nathaniel had only sarcasm for Jesus, whom he had never met. In contrast, Jesus had only good things to say about him.

Jesus' greeting in this passage seemed strange to me. It was not until I read further that I understood Jesus was setting up a contrast between Nathaniel and the Old Testament character Jacob, who is known as the "man of guile."

Nathaniel is understandably puzzled by Jesus' words. "How do you know me?" he asks.

And then came that piece of the puzzle that I had found in the book about the rabbis. Jesus answered, "I saw you while you were still under the fig tree before Phillip called you."

A simple response from Jesus to which we might expect the skeptical Nathaniel to respond, "So what?" But those seemingly ordinary words evoked the most remarkable reply from Nathaniel, who, in a moment, becomes no longer a skeptic but a follower. "Rabbi," he blurts out, "You are the Son of God; You are the King of Israel."[1]

The obvious question was: Why would Nathaniel change his mind so quickly because of such a simple statement? The key to the answer is that obscure fact: Rabbinic students prayed under fig trees. The rabbis had also said that "he who does not pray for the coming of the Messiah, does not pray at all."

I believe Nathaniel had been praying to see the coming

of the Messiah when Phillip called him there under the fig tree. People had begun to pray for the coming of the Messiah in Jesus' day, because of renewed messianic hopes raised by the teaching of the Pharisees. In light of Nathaniel's fantastic response to Jesus' simple statement, I believe he must have been praying for the Messiah to come at that very moment. Jesus knew two facts about Nathaniel: where he was praying and what he was praying for. Anyone might have known that he was under the fig tree, but only God could have known the subject of his prayer.

But what about that obscure comparison to Jacob, the man of guile? Jesus' final words in the story drive the point home in a powerful way. "You believe because I told you I saw you under the fig tree. You shall see greater things than that. I tell you the truth, you shall all see heaven open, and the angels of God ascending and descending on the Son of Man."

Jesus now refers to Jacob's fantastic dream.[2] What

Jacob, the man of guile, had only dreamed about, Nathaniel the guileless man would actually see. Jesus is Jacob's dream come true!

Everyone sees the footnote to Genesis 28 when they read the story of Jesus and Nathaniel, but to have all the pieces come together in such a perfect way! This was the first major breakthrough I was ever blessed with in my study of the Word, to see all at once the connection between the guileless Nathaniel and Jacob, the man of guile, and to understand that the stairway in the dream had become a person in Christ Jesus, the Way!

It was the first time a puzzling passage had come alive for me as a result of some digging. It is impossible to describe the feeling unless you have had the same experience. All I can say is I felt as if I had found a great treasure, which, of course, I had. The natural response for me was not to try to reduce it to written words, as I have finally tried to do here, but to sing about it. And I must confess that after reading back over the explanation, it does seem a bit more boring than singing the song!

LIGHT OF THE WORLD

You are the Light of the World, Oh, Lord,
And You make Your servants shine.
So how could there be any darkness in me
If You are the Light of the World?
If You are the Light of the World?

You are the Bread of Life, Oh, Lord,
Broken to set me free.
So how could there be any hunger in me
If You are the Bread of Life?
If You are the Bread of Life?

Wipe every tear away, Oh, Lord,
And teach us the song of the Lamb.
Your promise is true but it's still up to You
To wipe every tear away,
To wipe every tear away.

THE PASSION

...He showed them His hands and feet.

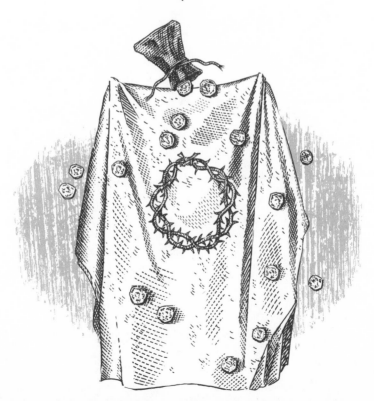

THE
PASSION

RIDE ON TO DIE

Sense the sorrow untold
As you look down the road
At the clamoring crowd drawing near.
Feel the heat of the day,
As you look down the way,
Hear the shouts of Hosanna the King.

Oh, daughter of Zion,
Your time's drawing near,
Don't forsake Him. Oh, don't pass it by.
On the foal of a donkey
As the prophets had said,
Passing by you, He rides on to die.

Come now, little foal,
Though you're not very old,
Come and bear your first burden bravely.
Walk so softly upon
All the coats and the palms,
Bear the One on your back, Oh, so gently.

Midst the shouting so loud,
And the joy of the crowd,
There is One who is riding in silence.
For He knows the ones here
Will be fleeing in fear
When their Shepherd is taken away.

Oh, daughter of Zion,
Your time's drawing near,
Don't forsake Him. Oh, don't pass it by.
On the foal of a donkey
As the prophets had said,
Passing by you, He rides on to die.

Soon the thorn-cursed ground
Will bring forth a crown,
And this Jesus will seem to be beaten.
But He'll conquer alone,
Both the shroud and the stone,
And the prophecies will be completed.

Oh, daughter of Zion,
Your time's drawing near;
Don't forsake Him. Oh, don't pass it by.
On the foal of a donkey
As the prophets had said,
Passing by you, He rides on to die.

The rabbis had said, "When the Messiah comes, if Israel is ready, He will come riding a white horse. But if Israel is not ready, He will ride a foal." When Jesus of Nazareth appeared outside Jerusalem on the afternoon of that tenth day of the month of Nisan, A.D. 33, he was riding a foal.

Jesus' final entry into the Holy City is usually referred to as the "Triumphal Entry," but that description really ignores many of the facts. There was, indeed, a commotion around Jesus, but it was hardly a triumph. His followers were excitedly laying down their coats for the little colt to walk on. They were waving palm branches they had cut outside Jericho, the "city of the palms," where Jesus had opened the eyes of Bartimaeus, who apparently followed Him along the road to Jerusalem.[1] It is not difficult to imagine that such a miracle would have stirred the crowd of pilgrims.

A few weeks earlier Jesus had raised His friend, Laza-

rus, from the dead. John tells us that the crowd was still talking about that miracle.[2] Lazarus himself might have been among this crowd, still being questioned and gawked at. Yet the excited followers of the Rabbi from Galilee were only a tiny speck in the huge herd of people crowding into Jerusalem for the Passover celebration. The "Triumphal Entry" was no more than a momentary uproar in the middle of a noisy crowd.

Preachers often speak of the fickleness of the crowd: On Monday they shouted, "Hosanna!" and on Friday, "Crucify Him!" That is a misunderstanding as well. The excited crowd around Jesus, the one that shouted, "Hosanna!" was comprised of His followers. The crowd that called out for His crucifixion later in the week was the "rabble" of Jerusalem, the cronies of the high priest, who were willing to do what they were asked no matter how despicable.

There are many misunderstandings concerning the final entry into Jerusalem, but the focus of the misconceptions is Jesus Himself. He is the misunderstood Messiah.

How can we call it the "Triumphal Entry" when Jesus was still wiping tears from His eyes? Luke describes the spot along the road to Jerusalem where the terrain rises and provides the first panorama of Jerusalem. Seeing the Holy City for the first time, the pilgrims would customarily break into joyful praise. Yet Luke tells us Jesus didn't sing. He wept.

There are two Greek words for crying. One of them is based on the word for *tear (∂akru)* and brings to mind the image of a single tear rolling down the cheek. It is the word for weeping silently inside yourself. That word is used in the story of Lazarus when "Jesus wept."[3]

The other word for crying sounds much like our own word for it *(klaio)*. It refers to weeping out loud, to "boo-hooing." This is the word that Luke uses to describe Jesus

weeping over Jerusalem. He literally sobbed over the city. There was little time to recover before the final entry.

The disciples talked about thrones on the way to Jerusalem, even though Jesus had been talking about crosses. The crowd shouted out, "Blessed is He who comes in the name of the Lord!" which was the usual greeting that was given to every pilgrim who had come to Passover. Yet Jesus was not just any pilgrim. The disciples were singing. Jesus was weeping. The disciples thought Israel was ready for the Messiah, but Jesus was riding a colt.

Jesus' first coming was characterized by misunderstanding. But there will be a Second. The misunderstood Messiah, who that day was a Lamb, will return as a Lion. *Every* eye will see Him then, and not simply a few followers in a crowd. No one will misunderstand. It will be the end of the world—and the beginning. Jesus will not be wiping tears of sorrow from His eyes but most likely tears of joy and relief. And He will be wiping away our tears as well. This time there will indeed be thrones. Revelation tells us Jesus will be riding a white horse. Does it mean we will be ready?

COME TO THE TABLE

Come to the table
And savor the sight,
The wine and the bread that was broken.
And all have been welcome to come
If they might,
Accept as their own these two tokens.
The bread is His body.
The wine is the blood.
And the One who provides them is true.
He freely offers.
We freely receive.
To accept and believe Him is all we must do.

Come to the table
And taste of the glory
And savor the sorrow;
He's dying tomorrow.
The hand that is breaking the bread
Soon will be broken.
And here at the table
Sit those who have loved Him,
One is a traitor and one will deny,
Though He's lived His life for them all
And for all be crucified.

Come to the table.
He's prepared for you
The bread of forgiveness, the wine of release.
Come to the table and sit down beside Him.
The Savior wants you to join in the feast.

Come to the table
And see in His eyes
The love that the Father has spoken.

And know you are welcome,
Whatever your crime,
Though every commandment you've broken.
For He's come to love you
And not to condemn,
And He offers a pardon of peace.
If you'll come to the table,
You'll feel in your heart
The greatest forgiveness,
The greatest release.

Come to the table
And taste of the glory
And savor the sorrow;
He's dying tomorrow.
The hand that is breaking the bread
Soon will be broken.
And here at the table
Sit those who have loved Him,
One is a traitor and one will deny,
Though He's lived His life for them all
And for all be crucified.

Come to the table
He's prepared for you
The bread of forgiveness, the wine of release.
Come to the table and sit down beside Him.
The Savior wants you to join in the feast.

I t was a Sunday morning, like any other during those college days. I had been up studying late the night before, so I was late getting to church. It was a small building, more than one hundred years old, located on the "declining side" of Bowling Green, Kentucky. Cecelia Memorial Presbyterian Church, named after Cecelia Lilliard, a freed slave who came back to Kentucky after the Civil War, started a college for young black women, and founded this church. A picture of her hung in the back of the church. She was a tiny woman, but the gleam in her eye told you she was the kind of woman you would expect to be the founder of two institutions at a time in history when all odds were against her.

I can remember the exact spot where I sat that particular morning. As so often happened, none of the congregation was prepared (nor could have been prepared) for what the Lord was about to do to us that morning. How do you prepare yourself for an encounter with God?

I noticed that the simple communion service was set up on the altar in front. "So today is communion," I muttered to myself. "I need it."

Our pastor, Bill Lane, got up to preach. He was very much the classical "rhetor"—marvelous to listen to, wonderfully articulate, and always challenging. He began talking about sin. The theological wheels in my head began to turn, responding, interacting, even challenging his various points. Then, quite unexpectedly, he began to list particular sins. That was "hitting below the belt." To discuss theologically the ramifications of sin and the obligatory sacrifice of Jesus is permissible, but to actually, concretely talk about sin!

Dr. Lane began by saying, "There are young couples in the congregation this morning who are not married but who have nonetheless spent the night together."

I looked around and realized that he was right. Many

of them were my friends. Dr. Lane's list went on and on—from the more blatant to the more subtle. With his wonderful skill with language he made the subtler sins sound just as sinful as the more blatant ones, which of course they were.

The feeling of guilt and conviction was heavy in the air. But Bill continued. When he finally came to the end, he repeated the list again in a condensed form, just to drive the nail all the way into our hearts.

The congregation was visibly shaken. Mostly young college students, we were not yet calloused grown-ups who might have weathered his attack better. Quite frankly, we were, most of us, numb.

After Dr. Lane's second volley, it seemed as if he were going to go through the list yet a third time. "If you are guilty of such and such, or this sin or that," he said as we all braced ourselves, "If you are guilty . . ." he paused, "If you are guilty, then this table is for you." With that Bill Lane pointed to the communion table in front of the pulpit. The service setting seemed to be bathed in light, its simplicity almost painful to look at.

At the very moment when we all thought Dr. Lane was going to push us into the pit we had all dug for ourselves, he threw us a rope. The table of the Lord. It was for us. For the couples who had "shacked up," for the students who had cheated and lied to pass a test, for the young men who had given up the battle with lust and given themselves to pornographic desires, for the druggies, for the thieves—for all of us, there it was. The bread and the cup. His body. "For I did not come to judge the world, but to save it," Jesus said.[1] His words really were true!

I felt the desire to rush to the table and seize the elements, like someone who had been lost in the wilderness, who was ravenously hungry and desperately thirsty. And

so I was, we all were, starving for Him. For the first time in my life communion became "Holy Communion." It meant life, not just a symbolic gesture to sit and be serious about. Communion now meant life and peace and joy. The rough hands of one of the elderly black deacons now placed a treasure worth selling everything for before me in those simple communion service pieces. It was all mine, for free!

Paul instructs us to sit in judgment upon ourselves, and that is what Dr. Lane helped each one of us to do that morning. For the first time I realized that the call to examine our sins before we take communion was not placed there so that we can somehow make a full accounting of our sins and thereby be worthy to come to the table. That call to judge ourselves helps us to realize that we have no right whatsoever to be there! You and I, we are the prostitutes and the tax collectors Jesus welcomed to fellowship with Him. The lunatic joy I felt only comes from seeing clearly that we have no right coming to the table at all.

Jesus, nonetheless, welcomes you and me as His special guests, to be astounded at His generosity.

In His wonderful parable of the feast, Jesus spoke of the rich man who gave a party and invited his friends, all of whom gave lame excuses for not coming. After some attempts to get a crowd together, the rich man instructed his servants to go out and "beat the bushes" to get someone, anyone, to come and share the incredible feast he had prepared. And, of course, the motley bunch who rolled out of the bushes is us!

After the benediction some time elapsed before we were able to get up. I remember my friend, Chuck, looking over at me, somewhat dazed, and asking, "Is it over?"

Well, it wasn't over. It had just begun.

Our experience that Sunday morning was a part of the special blessing Jesus grants to the ones who believe without actually seeing Him. I wonder if it's possible that communion meant more to us that morning than the Last Supper did to the Twelve, who were the first to receive the bread and cup from His own rough hands, two thousand years ago.

IN THE GARDEN

Trembling with fear,
Alone in the garden,
Battle before the final war.
Blood became tears,
There in the garden,
To fall upon the silent stones.

There in the darkness,
The light and the darkness
Stood still,
Two choices, one tortured will.
And there, once the choice had been made,
All the world could be saved,
By the One in the garden.

The light of the dawn
Was seen in the garden,
By gentle eyes,
So sadly wise.
The angels appear,
They come to the garden,
Clothed with sighs,
They realize.

The One they've adored from the start
Will be broken apart
By the ones He had come to save.
So they're here,
Simply now to be near.
He's no longer alone.
*They sit by Him and moan.**

Matthew 26:36ff.

When Jesus was arrested in Gethsemane, He was already bloody before anyone laid a hand on Him. He had been fighting a battle that would make certain the final outcome on Calvary. Without Gethsemane, there would have been no Golgotha. The blood and water that flowed from His wounds on the cross were preceded by bloody sweat that poured from His pores as He suffered the agony of a death more painful than the physical death on the cross, the death of the will.

Gethsemane literally means "place of crushing," a place where olives were crushed for their oil. That name took on an infinitely deeper meaning when Jesus knelt down there to pray that night in the garden. He was both a man and a child in Gethsemane. Full of courage, it was a man who faced not an uncertain death, but one that was fully known to Him. Jesus looked the Father in the face with mature, though anguished, honesty and said, "If there is any way for this cup to pass, let it be so!" The torment of the garden was the confrontation between the Son, whose perfect obedience came crashing against the human desire to say, "My will be done!" Jesus began to die in the garden.

Did Jesus want to go to the cross? The garden of Gethsemane tells us, no. Obedience is perfected not in doing something you want to do but in doing the last thing in the world you want to do. That is why His sweat flowed with blood. A man knelt in the garden, a man of unspeakable courage and obedience. A Man of Sorrows. . . .

Yet a child also knelt down there to pray. We hear the tones of a child in Jesus' plea, "Abba, anything is possible for you!" Jesus' words sound like a child's cry to his father for help, not a theological statement about an all-powerful Universal Being. (Every father is, at least for a little while, omnipotent to his children.) He was a child, screaming in the darkness, as if he were having a nightmare, only this was not a dream.

Jesus cried out, "Abba."

Never let anyone clothe that word in theological sophistication. It is not a sophisticated word! It is baby talk. Papa, Daddy, Abba—they are all the same thing: the first stutterings of an infant, not to be categorized in some systematic theological structure, but to be cried out from the heart of a child, a heart of faith.

Much has been said about the suffering of the cross: the physical, the emotional, and the spiritual agony. The agony of the cross, the crushing torment of it, was the separation Jesus experienced from the Father, the result of His obedience. That painful crushing began, appropriately enough, in the garden called Gethsemane.

TRAITOR'S LOOK

How did it feel to take the place
Of honor at the meal,
To take the sop from His own hands,
A prophecy to seal?
Was it because He washed your feet
That you sold Him as a slave,
The Son of Man, the Lamb of God,
Who'd only come to save?

The silver that they paid to you,
From out their precious till,
Was meant to buy a spotless Lamb,
A sacrifice to kill.
How heavy was the money bag
That couldn't set you free?
It became a heavy millstone
As you fell into the sea.

Now, Judas, don't you come too close.
I fear that I might see.
The traitor's look upon your face
Might look too much like me.
'Cause just like you I've sold the Lord,
And often for much less.
And like a wretched traitor,
I betrayed Him with a kiss.

In the ancient world there was a custom we recognize today: The honored guest sat at the right hand of the host. There was another tradition, which has been lost: The seat on the left side of the host was reserved for "the intimate friend." By our best reckoning, the disciple John was seated at Jesus' right hand at the Last Supper. Judas was at his left, the place reserved for the closest friend!

If Judas was an especially close friend of Jesus, the Gospel writers did their best to forget this. They developed a seething distaste for Judas, most often referring to him by some circumlocution like, "The one who betrayed Him." The Psalms employ another indirect and surprising name for Judas. In Psalm 41 he is called, "my close friend."

We love to speculate about Judas. Most "Jesus" movies give him the benefit of the doubt. Even the finest movie on the life of Christ, in my opinion, *Jesus of Nazareth* makes Judas out to be a helpless pawn, one who was really trying his best to force Jesus' hand and make Him prove to those in authority that He was truly the Messiah. From that perspective, Judas was not evil, he was confused.

Stop and think about that for a moment. Was it a confused man who came to the high priest on Wednesday of Passion Week and asked, "What are you willing to give me if I hand Him over to you?"[1] No, it was a thoroughly wicked man. Judas was willing to betray the Lord of the Universe for thirty pieces of silver, the rabbinic price for a slave! He was the living paradigm of the word *betrayer*. The incarnation of deceit.

What kind of person could have been with Jesus during those years of ministry and yet do such a thing? For at least two-and-a-half years, and probably three, Judas had heard Jesus speak of love and forgiveness, had watched Jesus flawlessly live out all that He had taught. No one had ever been exposed to such a teacher.

Judas engaged in Jesus' ministry. He was sent out with

the Twelve, paired up with Simon, the zealot.[2] Did Jesus place them together because Judas needed Simon's zeal or because Simon needed something Jesus thought Judas might have to offer? Or could it simply be because they were both zealots? (Some scholars believe that Iscariot might mean "man of the knife," another term for zealot.) When the disciples returned from their mission rejoicing that even the demons submitted to them, Judas must have been at least a little bit excited. I find it hard to believe that Judas spent all those years as a sinister shadow, waiting for the right moment to betray His Lord.

We might think that the Gospel writers avoided looking too closely at Judas because they did not want to dwell on someone like him. What's the use of looking at a man whose destiny was destruction? After all, who, in their right mind, would ever name their child Judas? He was evil, dark, a liar, a betrayer. His was the face of death. Who wants to look at a face like that?

But could there be another reason why no one likes looking at Judas? Do we avoid him because we fear that we might see someone familiar when we look in his tormented eyes? Ourselves, perhaps? Is that why we like to give him the benefit of the doubt and speculate that he was really manipulated by God into doing what he did? Wouldn't we really like to give ourselves the same benefit of the doubt and, in essence, blame God for our wrongdoing?

The biblical scholar J. I. Packer says that we all betray Jesus with a kiss. We have walked with Him, heard His voice. We have been His welcomed guests at His table, invited to sit at the left, His friends. He has washed our feet and more. Yet we often sell Him for far less than thirty pieces of silver. Our tendency is to slither up and plant a hypocritical kiss on His sweet lips, turning Him over to a world that would tear Him apart and crucify Him all over again.

Don't look away from Judas because Judas is you and me. His weaknesses are ours. His wickedness is ours. Look hard at him the next time you are tempted to manipulate people to get your own way. See if you don't recognize yourself.

Then look back again to the One who was betrayed, who was sold as a slave. Know that He isn't looking at you the same way you're looking at yourself. As far as He is concerned, the place of the intimate friend is still yours. Though we've all betrayed Him, He is ready to kiss us with gentle lips that whisper, "My friend."

WHY

Why did it have to be a friend
Who chose to betray the Lord?
And why did he use a kiss to show them?
That's not what a kiss is for.

Only a friend can betray a friend.
A stranger has nothing to gain.
And only a friend comes close enough
To ever cause so much pain.

And why did there have to be a thorny crown
Pressed upon His head?
It should have been a royal one,
Made of jewels and gold instead.

It had to be a crown of thorns
Because in this life that we live,
For all who would seek to love
A thorn is all the world has to give.

And why did it have to be a heavy cross
He was made to bear?
And why did they nail His feet and hands?
His love would have held Him there.

It was a cross, for on a cross
A thief was supposed to pay.
And Jesus had come into the world
To steal every heart away.
Yes, Jesus had come into the world
To steal every heart away.

The trappings of the crucifixion had always puzzled me:

• Why was it necessary that a close friend betray Jesus?

• Why the crown of thorns, that grim tribute to the humor of man? Was it really so vital to the final outcome?

• Why the cross? Couldn't there have been some other way for Him to die?

"Why?" is a faithless question. You might as well ask, "Why did my loved one have to die?" Or, "Why do the innocent suffer?" All these "whys" set the mind vainly running in circles.

Deitrich Bonhoeffer, the well-known theologian, says that the only question that really matters is "Who?" Not "When?" or "What?" or "Why?" Asking the question "Who?" leads us to Jesus.

Bonhoeffer is right, of course. "Why?" questions are ultimately of no use to the believer. So why did someone supposedly committed to asking "Who?" put so many "Why?" questions into a song?

I had been playing with these questions for quite some time, trying to make them sound lyrical, which is to say, trying to make them sound pretty. But they aren't pretty questions.

The three questions which make up the verses of the song were all finished. I had planned to write one chorus, which would answer all three. That proved to be as impossible as the questions themselves. So I did the only thing a committed seeker of the Truth could do: I gave up and put them away in a drawer!

Weeks later I was awakened in the night with the three separate choruses going through my mind, something that had never happened before—and has never happened

since. To my trilogy of vain, cynical questions the Lord gave three unexpected answers:

Why did it have to be a friend?
Only a friend comes close enough to cause such pain.
Why the thorny crown?
Because in this life, the only kind of crown the world would give such a Lover is a crown of thorns.
Why did it have to be a cross?
Because the cross is the place for a thief. And Jesus had come to steal the world's heart away.

Each time I listen to the song, I hear two separate voices. My own pessimistic voice, asking the meaningless "why" questions, and another gentler Voice, speaking the wonderful answers.

CROSS OF GLORY

From the pages of the prophets,
He stepped out into the world
And walked the earth in lowly majesty.
Though He had been Creator,
A creature now was He,
Come to bear love's sacred mystery.

He, the Truth, was called a liar.
The only Lover hated so.
He was many times a martyr before He died,
Forsaken by the Father,
Despised by all the world.
He alone was born to be the Crucified.

Upon the cross of glory,
His death was life to me,
A sacrifice of love's most sacred mystery.
And death rejoiced to hold Him,
Though soon He would be free.
For love must always have the victory.

Though no rhyme could ever tell it.
No words could ever say.
And no chord is foul enough to sing the pain.
Still we feel the burden
And suffer with your song.
You love us so but yet
You bid us sing.

Upon the cross of glory,
His death was life to me,
A sacrifice of love's most sacred mystery.
And death rejoiced to hold Him,

Though soon He would be free.
For love must always have the victory.

There it is on the communion table: the shiny brass crucifix. And there it is again on the lapel of the businessman, who wants his customers to know that he is a Christian. And again, hanging from the ear of a heavy metal singer. And in the corner of the business card of the Agape Plumbing Service. And on the steeple of a church, and on the bumper of a car, and in the hotel lobby, next to the Star of David, to show lodgers where they might worship if they care to. I went to school with a boy who had a cross tattooed under his eye. I was never sure what that meant. Sometimes I'm not so sure what the cross means in any of those other places either.

The pop singer, Madonna, says, "It's sexy to wear a crucifix because there is a naked man on it." Her statement reflects a sick movement in secular rock music to empty the cross of its meaning. It is a movement, unfortunately, that started in the American Christian church years ago. The cross used to stand for Jesus, and more precisely, the suffering of Jesus. Now it stands for an institution that most often doesn't really stand for anything other than the advancement of its own institutionality, its buildings and programs.

I have a small plastic replica of a panel from an ivory box in the British Museum, which dates around A.D. 200. This panel depicts Jesus on the cross in one corner and Judas, hanging himself, in the other. The craftsmanship is rather crude but the significance of the piece derives from something other than the artistic detail. It is the first known

representation of Jesus on the cross in Christian art, or any art for that matter. A.D. 200! More than one-hundred-and-fifty years after the crucifixion. It took the early Christians that long to finally get around to portraying Jesus on the cross.

The early Christians had other symbols, the fish or icthus. They sometimes even used the star of David, since most of them were Jewish.

Why didn't they utilize the symbol of the cross? Were they ashamed of it? Or were they merely embarrassed by it? Who can tell. My guess is that they shied away from representing the cross because it meant too much, not because it meant too little (as it does today). The cross was a symbol they cherished in their hearts. Maybe they desired that the cross become a vivid reality, which could only be kept alive in their hearts, instead of a symbol around their necks or below their eyes.

The cross is not a symbol. It is the center of the universe, the nexus of history, the most meaningful event that ever took place. Someone has even gone so far as to say that the crucifixion of Jesus is the only thing that ever really happened. Though the world, both pagan and Christian, seems bent on reducing the meaning of the cross, it is irreducible.

CROWN HIM!

"Crown Him! Crown Him!"
 The angry people cried.
"Crown Him! Crown Him!
 Let him be crucified!"

"Crown Him! Crown Him!
 Let Him not remain alive!"
"Crown Him! Crown Him!
 He must be crucified."

So a circle of pain and love
Came down upon His head. ("Crown Him!")
It was not for anything He'd done,
Nor for anything He'd said. ("Crown Him!")
For all His life He'd sought to show
They were only living a lie.
But they didn't care to hear or know,
They just wanted Him to die.

Soon the circle of glory
Will be placed upon His brow.
And He'll come to reign forever,
Though it may not seem so now.
And our time of tears and trouble
Will seem only like a dream
As we stand before the glory
Of our Savior and our King.

"Crown Him! Crown Him!"
 Holy angels sing.
"All glory, honor, power, and praise
 Will crown the King of Kings!"

"Crown Him! Crown Him!"
 Those redeemed and damned,

Will bow the knee and humbly
Sing, "Worthy is the Lamb."

First Samuel 8 contains one of the most heartbreaking scenes in the Old Testament. Here the Israelites reject God and ask, instead, for a human king. You can hear the pathos in God's voice as He tells Samuel, "Listen to all that the people are saying to you; it is not you they have rejected as their king, but Me."[1] When God finally sent His own Son to be their king, they crowned Him, not with gold, but with thorns.

It was meant to be a joke. The Roman soldiers, basically bored with their assignment on the fringes of the Empire, were looking for something to pass the time. When the crazy Rabbi from Nazareth was left in their hands, they had the chance to vent some of the frustration that had been building up ever since they had been assigned to this "god-forsaken place." It was just a joke, but they seem to be the only ones in all of history to see the humor in it.

When Jesus came from the soldiers' mocking, wearing the crown of thorns and the purple horse blanket, Pilate uttered the infamous, "Ecce homo!" "Behold the man!"

The crowd responded with shouts of, "Crucify Him!"

The people had pierced Jesus for years with their cruel words. Now they pierced Him with the thorns of a crown. "They will look on . . . the one they have pierced," Zechariah had prophesied.[2] Later they would see Him pierced again and again; with nails through His hands and feet, and finally with a spear thrust into His side. "He was pierced for our transgressions, He was crushed for our iniquities; the punishment that brought us peace was upon

Him, and by His wounds we are healed.''[3] The ground that had been cursed with thorns now brought forth a thorny crown for its unrecognized and rejected Creator.

That first crown, given to Jesus by the soldiers, is not the last, however. In fact, partly because of that crown, that mocking and that gruesome death, Jesus has received another crown. In his great revelation, John saw Jesus with other crowns on His head. "I saw heaven standing open and there before me was a white horse, whose rider is called Faithful and True. With justice He judges and makes war. His eyes are like blazing fire, and on His head are many crowns. . . . His name is the Word of God.''[4] The meek, thorn-crowned One, who first entered the Holy City riding a colt, will return riding upon a magnificent white horse, wearing not one, but many crowns. He who suffered so many injustices at the hands of men will return "with justice." His eyes, which before were so full of tears and pain, will blaze like fire. What Pilate had said with his own grim humor will be seen by the universe, after all, to be true! He is "King of Kings and Lord of Lords!"

In chapter 4 of Revelation John tells us that the "many crowns" on Jesus' head are those belonging to the elders seated around the throne of God. I can't help but believe that they are also the crowns we will be given: crowns of rejoicing, of righteousness, of life and glory. They too will be placed at Jesus' wounded feet. And the same ears that bore the angry shouts of the crowd will hear angels and the multitude of the faithful saying, "Crown Him with glory and honor and power!"

KNOWN BY THE SCARS

Mother Mary cried as she held heaven in her arms
For the shadow of the scar she saw was clear
As her own bewildered baby lay weeping for the world
Whose frightened tears would free us all from fear.

The marks of death that God chose never to erase,
The wounds of love's eternal mark,
When the kingdom comes, with its perfected sons,
He will be known by the scars.

For a time He sought to tell the world He was the way,
That God, the Father, had a human heart,
With His own holy hands He sought to touch and heal their scars
But they chose to tear those gentle hands apart.

No one was there to wipe away the tears
That burned the holy eyes of God
As He looked upon His one and only Son
Who'd never sinned or lied,
Yet was crucified.

The marks of death that God chose never to erase,
The wounds of love's eternal mark,
When the kingdom comes, with its perfected sons,
He will be known by the scars.

And after they had slain Him and laid Him in the grave,
The ones He loved had fled into the dark,
Then love and power raised Him.
And God won the victory
But they only recognized Him by the scars.

The marks of death, that God chose never to erase,
The wounds of love's eternal mark,

When the kingdom comes, with its perfected sons,
He will be known by the scars.

Joseph is a tall, slender man, like most Masai. He is a
warrior. His face bears the ritual scars every young
man receives after killing his first lion with only a
spear and shield. But the scars on his face and his ordeal
with the lion are not what make Joseph special.

He had made the long journey from Africa to Amster-
dam for the Itinerant Evangelists Conference, hoping for
the chance to meet Billy Graham, hoping to share with him
his incredible story. I learned about Joseph because my
friend, Robert, was responsible for screening Graham's visi-
tors. In the few days of the conference it would have been
impossible for all those who were wanting to meet Dr.
Graham to do so. But after the young African shared his
story with Robert, the meeting was quickly arranged.

The story began when Joseph, who was walking along
one of those hot, dusty African roads, met someone who
shared the good news of Jesus Christ with him. Then and
there he accepted Jesus as his Lord and Savior. The power
of the Spirit began transforming his life. He was filled with
such excitement and joy that the first thing he wanted to do
was return to his own village and share the good news with
the members of his local tribe.

Joseph began going door-to-door, telling everyone he
met about the cross of Jesus and the salvation it offered,
expecting to see their faces light up the way his had. To his
amazement the villagers not only didn't care, they became
hostile. The men of the village seized him, holding him to
the ground, while the women began to beat him with

strands of barbed wire. He was dragged from the village and left to die alone in the bush.

Joseph somehow managed to crawl to a water hole, and there, after two days of passing in and out of consciousness, found he had the strength to get up. He still wondered about the hostile reception he had received from the people he had known all his life. He decided he must have left something out or told the story of Jesus wrong. After rehearsing the message he had first heard he decided to go back to the village and share his faith once more.

Joseph limped back into the circle of huts and began again to proclaim the good news about Jesus. "He died for you, so that you might find forgiveness and come to know the living God," he pleaded. Once again he was grabbed by the men of the village and held while the women beat him a second time, opening up wounds that had only just begun to heal. Once more they dragged him, unconscious, from the village and left him to die.

To have survived the first beating was truly remarkable. To live through the second was a miracle. Again, days later, Joseph awoke in the wilderness, bruised and scarred and yet determined to go back.

For the third time he returned to the small village. This time he found everyone waiting for him. They attacked him before he even had a chance to open his mouth. As they began to flog him for the third and probably last time, he began again to speak to them of Jesus Christ, the Lord, who had the power to forgive sin and give them new life. The last thing he remembered before he passed out was seeing the women who were beating him begin to weep.

This time he awoke in his own bed, not in the wilderness. The very ones who had so severely beaten him were now trying to save his life and nurse him back to health. The entire village had come to Christ.

Joseph, after telling his story, lifted his colorful, flowing

African shirt to show my friend and Dr. Graham the scars-upon-scars that covered his chest and back. After thanking them both for listening, he turned and walked away.

Robert told me all Dr. Graham could say was, "I'm not fit to untie his shoes, and he wanted to meet me?"

Joseph is not known by the ritual scars he bears on his face, nor by his achievement as a Masai warrior. He is recognized by the scars he incurred from faithfully following Jesus to the point of death.

Something unusual happened after the Resurrection of Jesus. No one recognized him. Mary, in the garden outside His empty tomb, thought He was the gardener. It wasn't until He spoke her name, "Mary," that she realized who He was. She recognized Him by His voice.

The disciples on the road to Emmaus walked and talked a long time with Jesus, long enough for Him to explain everything in the Old Testament concerning Himself. (And that must have taken a long time!) Yet those two disciples didn't recognize Jesus either. Later that same after-

noon they coerced Him into sharing a meal with them. It wasn't until Jesus broke the bread that the Bible says their eyes were opened. At that instant He vanished.

Mary recognized His familiar voice. The disciples at Emmaus recognized Him in the breaking of the bread. The weary fishermen knew it was Him because of a miraculous catch. We, too, can recognize the resurrected Jesus in all these ways, by His voice, at His Table, by the miracles He still performs.

When Jesus wanted to be recognized the first thing the Bible says He did was show them His scars. He didn't point to His face and say, "Look, it's Me." He showed them His hands and feet and side and gently said, "Look, it's Me." Jesus is known by His scars.

The prophet Zechariah asked Jesus in a vision, "Where did you get those wounds?" Jesus responded, "This is where I was wounded for My friends."[1]

At the far end of history, John, weeping because no one could open the special scroll, was told by an elder standing beside him in the heavenly crowd, "Do not weep. Behold, the Lion of the tribe of Judah."[2]

John looked up, expecting to see a lion. But what did he see? A Lamb. And he knew who that Lamb was precisely because it was wounded.

Jesus is known by His scars. When we stand in His presence He won't point to His face but to His scars and say, "Look, it's Me!"

Modern-day heretics point to material wealth and say, "Look, it's Jesus!" But the true followers of all ages, from the long forgotten martyrs to that beautiful young Masai will tell you, "This is Jesus, for I bear in my own body the marks of His death."[3] As Jesus' resurrected body was recognized by its scars, so His body, the church, should be known by its scars and tears and the unspeakable joy it knows in spite of, and indeed because of, it all.

175

HERE I STAND

As I stand before the glory,
As I look upon the pain,
As I hear the sound of sorrow in the wind,
As the earth begins to tremble
Does it wonder?
What's the use of turning if Jesus'
Eyes are growing dim?

Enveloped in the darkness,
Surrounded by the night,
Could it be that life is death,
And death is really life?
The only hope for meaning
The simple question why?
To be witness to the paradox
That God's about to die.

In this world of blind illusion,
Where the truth is called a lie,
As we stumble through the way of life,
How could You be my guide?
Do You really want my hopeless heart?
Do You long to love me so?
As I stand before the cross of love,
How can I answer no?

Amidst Your awful pain
I sense an overwhelming peace.
Beyond the nails and bonds
I see victorious release.
Unlike You I'm bound to time,
So I must live within the years.
I would long to come and be with You
And suffer through Your tears.

In this world of blind illusion,
Where the truth is called a lie,
As we stumble through the way of life,
How could You be my guide?
Do You really want my hopeless heart?
Do You long to love me so?
As I stand before the cross of love,
How can I answer no?

I t was an unusually warm day for early February. I had come into our small town to do a few errands, and especially to get a little gift for my wife. At the last minute, our friend Dan had given us tickets for a play, so I was trying to arrange as special an evening as I could on such short notice. I finally decided on a corsage, the kind boys used to give girls on prom night. That's what I wanted our date to feel like, prom night.

Our town, Franklin, was the scene of one of the bloodiest battles of the Civil War. Since the state did not have the funds to buy property on the battlefield, there is no state park here to commemorate the battle as there are for many other battles that were much smaller in scale. All that's here is a museum called "The Carter House," a small house that actually survived being located in the center of the battle. The Carter House still stands today, on Columbia Pike, a despairingly small monument to a very bloody battle.

Almost seven thousand men died in the immediate vicinity of that house in a battle that lasted only five hours. The Federal troops used up one hundred wagon loads of ammunition in that short time. I've read accounts of bodies being stacked six and seven deep for more than a mile

along Columbia Pike. Even the most hardened soldiers said after the battle that they had never seen anything like it.

The flower shop that had my corsage is located next door to the Carter House. When I placed my order the lady at the desk said that it would be fifteen or twenty minutes before my flowers would be ready. It was such a beautiful day outside I decided to go into the yard of the shop and wait.

Two of the original outbuildings are still standing beside the Carter House. They are peppered with bullet holes on the sides of the buildings that faced the battle. On the opposite sides are the exit holes. I walked over to one of the small reddish buildings and examined the evidence of the battle. The main earth works (trenches dug by the Federal troops where the center of the battle was fought) passed directly through what is now the side yard of the flower shop. The fiercest part of the battle had raged right where I was standing. You can still make out a slight indentation in the ground. That shallow dip in the earth is all that is left. Hundreds of bodies were simply left in these trenches when they were filled in, a mass burial.

As I stood beside the wall of the small structure, looking at what little physical evidence of the battle was left, I was struck by the most profound realization of what had really happened there. The horror and the blood. The screams of the wounded and dying. Seven thousand of them! I could almost see the bodies strewn there, hear the cries for water, the sounds of wounded men and horses. The loss of so many young lives. So many families destroyed. The bitterness of such defeat still hangs on in some pockets of the South.

The scars of the battle have all but been erased. Flowers grow where the lines once were. One of the workers showed me human teeth that had just surfaced the day before after a long rain.

"It happens all the time," he said nonchalantly.

Across the street is a pizza place and some small shops. High school kids gather and eat pizza where hundreds of men brutally lost their lives. I kept asking myself, *How could this happen? How could such a mountain of pain and suffering ever be covered up, erased, and all but forgotten? How could men build flower shops and pizza stands on such hallowed ground?*

As I was driving home, still somewhat dazed and with Susan's corsage now safely in tow, a second, no less powerful realization struck me. I had been so awestruck in that back yard that was once a battlefield, and yet everyday I stand before a token of suffering, which overshadows that forgotten battle as a mountain overshadows a grain of sand. It is the cross, of course.

There must have been a time in my life when I was awestruck by the cross in the same way I was that day beside the flower shop. But, God forgive me, I can't remember when it was.

Perhaps we do not grasp the magnitude of the cross because we cannot possibly hope to grasp it. We dwell on the physical agony of Jesus, the nails and the thorns, but they make up only the most minute portion of His suffering. There are people alive today that have suffered such pain, and even more. What cannot be grasped by any living soul is the spiritual and emotional agony of Jesus. It is impossible.

The cross was the only moment in all eternity when Jesus was separated from the Father. They had always been One. But now, quite unimaginably, They were separated by our sin.

Jesus cried out, "Why have You forsaken Me?" precisely because God did forsake Him there. As the pure and spotless Lamb of God became sin for you and me, the Father had to look away, for the Bible tells us that His eyes are too holy to look upon sin.[1] On the cross, for the only

time in eternity, the Father took His eyes off the Son as the Son's tear-filled eyes looked for the Father.

When the creeds say that Jesus descended into hell, that is what they mean. Hell is separation from God, separation from everything that is good, that is life and light. Hell is the price to pay for sin. And so that is what Jesus paid. The darkness that covered Him there on Golgotha wasn't an atmospheric phenomenon as much as it was a spiritual reality. In one sense the darkness must have radiated from Jesus, not around Him. For if darkness is the visible manifestation of sin, and Jesus became sin on the cross for you and me, then the darkness that covered Him there was as much from Him as around Him. He who was the Light became darkness on the cross. Jesus, who was the Life, not only became dead on the cross, but became in some sense Death itself.

In some indescribable way, the death of one man can be more significant, more moving, than the death of a thousand. At the battle of Franklin the youngest son of the Carters, a boy named Todd, was killed almost in his own front yard, trying to make it home. Today he is spoken of and written about more than the other 6,999 men who also lost their lives that day. The poignant situation of his death somehow seems to eclipse the others.

What about the Son of Man, whose unspeakable death speaks more than a mountain of pain? As we stand before the cross, we should feel as if we are standing upon a battlefield, the ground still wet with blood and pain. The screams, His cries of thirst, should still ring our ears. And what small part of that spiritual battle we can grasp, we must hold on to for all our lives because we were a part of the reason for it. If we belong to Him, we are now a part of the battle itself and it is a part of us.

THIS MUST BE THE LAMB

On a gray April morning as a chilling wind blew,
A thousand dark promises were about to come true.
As Satan stood trembling, knowing now he had lost,
As the Lamb took His first step on the way to the cross.

This must be the Lamb,
The fulfillment of all God had spoken.
This must be the Lamb,
Not a single bone will be broken.
Like a sheep to the slaughter,
So silently still,
This must be the Lamb.

They mocked His true calling and laughed at His fate,
So glad to see the Gentle One consumed by their hate.
Unaware of the wind and the darkening sky,
So blind to the fact that it was God limping by.

This must be the Lamb,
The fulfillment of all God had spoken.
This must be the Lamb,
Not a single bone will be broken.
Like a sheep to the slaughter,
So silently still,
This must be the Lamb.

The poor women weeping at what seemed a great loss,
Trembling in fear there at the foot of the cross.
Tormented by memories that came like a flood,
Unaware that their pardon must be bought by His blood.

This must be the Lamb,
The fulfillment of all God had spoken.
This must be the Lamb,
Not a single bone will be broken.

Like a sheep to the slaughter,
So silently still,
This must be the Lamb.

I t was John the Baptist who first recognized Jesus as
the "Lamb of God." "Behold! The Lamb of God who
takes away the sin of the world!" he shouted as Jesus
approached.[1] The sacrificial "seal of approval" had already
been placed on Jesus.[2]

The Old Testament says a lot about sacrificial lambs.
The children of Israel sacrificed them and painted the doorposts of their houses in Egypt with the blood so the angel
of death would "Passover" their houses.[3] In the New Testament Jesus is our Passover Lamb.[4] We mark the doorposts
of our hearts, as it were, with His blood so the angel that is
the second death will "Passover" us.

One of the details of the offering of the Passover lamb
was that none of its bones were to be broken.[5] It was per-
mitted to pull the carcass apart at the joint, but the bones
were to be kept intact. When Jesus is crucified the apostle
John is moved by the fact that His bones were kept from
being broken. The Jews did not want the bodies of the
three crucified men left on the crosses during their Passover.
They were afraid it might dampen the celebration! They
went to Pilate with an almost unbelievably gruesome request. Because the prisoners had to be dead before they
were taken down, and there was a good chance that all
three were still alive, (crucifixion usually took days to kill a
victim), the priests asked that the legs of the three crucified
men be broken so that their deaths might be hurried along.

The Romans used a heavy wooden mallet to break the

two lower leg bones, causing the full weight of the body to be brought to bear on the chest, causing a quicker death by suffocation. As horrible a death as crucifixion was, it is hard to think of how it might have been made worse. But the breaking of the legs, though bringing about a more immediate death, must have been excruciating. (The Latin root for *excruciating* is the word for *cross*.)

The two thieves on either side of Jesus were apparently still alive. Like most other victims of crucifixion, they would probably have lasted for days. The soldiers broke the legs of both men. When they came to Jesus, however, they discovered that He was already dead. He had "dismissed" His spirit with the words of Psalm 31:5, "Into your hands I commit my spirit." (He had earlier quoted Psalm 22:1.) Since He was already dead, there was no need for the soldiers to break His legs. The prophecy of Psalm 34:20, "He protects all His bones, not one of them will be broken," was perfectly fulfilled. To make sure Jesus was dead, the soldiers pierced His side with a spear, causing blood and water from the broken sack around His heart to flow.

Three years earlier in that uncluttered countryside, when John had shouted across the Jordan, "Behold the Lamb of God," who would have ever thought it would mean this?

LOVE CRUCIFIED AROSE

Long ago He blessed the earth,
Born older than the years.
And in the stall a cross He saw
Through the first of many tears.
A life of homeless wandering,
Cast out in sorrow's way,
The Shepherd seeking for the lost,
His life the price He'd pay.

Love crucified arose.
The risen One in splendor,
Jehovah's soul defender,
Has won the victory.
Love crucified arose.
And the grave became a place of hope,
For the heart that sin and sorrow broke
Is beating once again.

Throughout Your life You felt the weight
Of what You'd come to give.
To drink for us that crimson cup,
So we might really live.
At last the time to love and die,
The dark appointed day,
That one forsaken moment when
Your Father turned His face away.

Love crucified arose.
The One who lived and died for me
Was Satan's nail-pierced casualty,
Now He's breathing once again.
Love crucified arose.
And the grave became a place of hope,

For the heart that sin and sorrow broke
Is beating once again.

Love crucified arose.
The risen One in splendor,
Jehovah's soul defender,
Has won the victory.
Love crucified arose.
And the grave became a place of hope,
For the heart that sin and sorrow broke
Is beating once again.

When I was in high school, I worked for a while for an ambulance company, which was owned, oddly enough, by a funeral home. I worked from midnight until eight in the morning. That meant a lot of waiting around and listening to police radios to see if we could beat the other ambulances to accident sites. (A pretty ghoulish thing to do as I look back on it.) From time to time I was asked to help clean up in the "front," or funeral parlor section of the building. This meant that I had many chances to view bodies that either were in caskets or lying on tables in the "prep" room, waiting to be put out for "viewing." (I have since decided to be cremated!) Usually, this was in the middle of the night, a time when the imagination is somewhat more active, alone in a room with a dead body.

Over and over, when looking at a deceased body, one thought kept repeating itself in my mind: "There is no way in the world this person is ever going to get up again!" It is one thing to talk about resurrection in a seminary class-

room or Bible study. It's another to stand before prospective "resurrectees" and claim that they will rise again. Yet Jesus Christ did just that. He rose from the dead!

The simple details in John's account of the contents of Jesus' tomb are fascinating. Whenever a detail is given in Scripture there is a purpose. (For instance, Luke tells us it was Malchus's "little ear" or earlobe that Peter cut off, so we can reconstruct what happened there in the garden of Gethsemane: Peter was trying to cut off his head, not his ear! The slave turned just in the nick of time and lost only his earlobe. John gives us the detail that the baskets used to gather up the leftovers at the feeding of the five thousand were the small, "lunch pail" variety, so we learn that the point was not that there was an abundance of food left over, but exactly enough to provide for the twelve disciples, who, as servants, were entitled to collect the "peah" or leftovers.)

The first person to see the contents of the tomb was John. (The women who had been there earlier had seen two angels but didn't notice the contents of the burial chamber.) Because John was younger than Peter, he could outrun him, and so he was the first to arrive, bend over, and look inside.

John saw two objects: the strips of linen that had been wrapped around the body and the cloth that had been wrapped around Jesus' face. He tells us that the strips of linen were simply "lying there" but gives the interesting detail that the facial cloth was folded up, separate from the linen.

These details seem to point to the fact that at the moment of Jesus' resurrection there was an absence of haste. He took the time to unwrap the cloth from around His face and fold it up, laying it aside separately from the linen strips, which His body seems to have simply passed through.

The details of the articles in the tomb cause me to imagine what the moment of the Resurrection might have been like. A picture that repeatedly comes to mind is that of Jesus' heart, which had been still since Friday, beginning to beat again. His chest expands, and begins steadily to rise and fall. His eyes slowly open beneath the facial cloth. Jesus is alive again!

The fact of Jesus' resurrection is the reason for our hope that we will rise again as well.[1] I wonder if there will be the same absence of haste when my own eyes, though dust and ashes, slowly open to finally see His face.

HE WAS HEARD

In the days of old
The priest would come
With a lifeless sacrifice,
While the crowd in anxious silence
Would wait outside.
As he entered in the temple,
They only hoped he would be heard.
God would give them a tomorrow,
And the priest would stay alive.

Their only chance,
Their only hope,
Would he be heard?
The only way
They might be saved,
Would he be heard?

In the fullness of the promised time,
The final Priest did come
And He offered up a living sacrifice.
Now we His children wait for Him
With hope and joyful praise,
For we know that God has heard Him,
For we know that He was raised.

He offered
Tearful prayers
And He was heard.
He offered up
His life
And He was heard.

So let us fix our eyes upon
The Priest whom God did hear.

For the joy that was before Him,
He overcame the fear.
For once and all He paid the cost,
Enduring all the shame,
Taking up the cruel cross,
Ignoring all the pain.

The crowd is waiting outside the temple in silence. The signal has already been given. The high priest has gone into the Holy of Holies and, for the only time in the year allowed, has spoken the sacred name of God. At that signal the Jews assembled outside in the courtyard fall to their faces in respect and fear, since the priest and presumably the temple will be destroyed if he has spoken "the name" with impure lips.

The crowd awaits the high priest's return to the front of the temple with the announcement that the sacrifice has been accepted and that full forgiveness has been granted. The sacrifice he offers is for his sins and for the sins of the people. If he returns, all is well. If he does not return, the crowd outside will know that he has been struck down in the temple and they will remain guilty, unclean, hopeless. He is their only hope.

In the book of Hebrews, the writer presents Jesus as our High Priest. The high priest in the Old Testament offered up blood that was "not his own," a lifeless sacrifice, but Jesus offered His own blood. His sacrifice was better because it was a living sacrifice, which was offered "once for all," not every year. And unlike the high priest, who served only for a specific period of time, Jesus' is an eternal priesthood (the order of Melchizedek).[1]

Even as Jesus is our High Priest, so we are in the same position as those early Israelites. We wait expectantly, but without fear, for our High Priest's return, for, "He will appear a second time, not to bear sin, but to bring salvation to those who are waiting for Him."[2] The relief the children of Israel had at seeing their high priest return is nothing in comparison to the relief we will have at seeing the clouds roll back and Jesus, our High Priest, appear again.

(These lyrics and this devotion are based on a lecture by Dr. William Lane. This information will appear in his upcoming commentary on the book of Hebrews.)

STRANGER ON THE SHORE

In the early morning mist they saw a stranger on the seashore.
He somehow seemed familiar asking what the night had brought.
With taut anticipation then they listened to His order
And pulling in the net found more than they had ever caught.

The one He loved first recognized the stranger there was Jesus.
He alone remembered this had happened once before.
The one who had denied Him, who had once walked on the water,
Jumped in and swam to Him, to be confronted on the shore.

You need to be confronted by the stranger on the shore.
You need to have Him search your soul, you need to hear the call.
You need to learn exactly what it means for you to follow.
You need to realize that He's asking for it all.

The meal He had prepared for them was waiting on the fire,
The smell of bread, the sizzle of the fish upon the coals.
The laughter and the joy at once more being all together,
They didn't realize that He was searching all their souls.

Then came the painful questions that would pierce the soul of Simon,
A threefold chance to reaffirm the love he had denied.
The gentle eyes which saw his heart and waited for an answer,
Had seen the look upon his face the moment he had lied.

You need to be confronted by the stranger on the shore.
You need to have Him search your soul, you need to hear the call.
You need to learn exactly what it means for you to follow.
You need to realize that He's asking for it all.

Now realize that you must face and answer all His questions,
As you stand before the stranger on the shore inside your heart.
Is a threefold chance enough to do away with your betrayals?
Or should you ask the stranger if He'll give you a new start?*

---

*John 21:1–14.

It seems odd that the disciples returned to fishing after Jesus' resurrection. Yet that's just what they did. Perhaps it was because fishing was all they knew and having left everything to follow Jesus, they had to fish to survive. They had been out all night long and hadn't caught a single fish. (It's a good thing Jesus called them to be His disciples, because they didn't seem to be very good fishermen!)

As the disciples guided their boat to the shore—their hearts as empty as their nets—they saw a stranger standing on the sand, watching them from the shore.

The stranger asked a pointed question, a question which in Greek expects the answer "No." "Children, you haven't caught any fish, have you?"

"No," the disciples shouted back.

"Throw your net on the right side of the boat and you will find some," said the stranger, pointing to the exact spot.

All of a sudden the net was overflowing!

The disciple John, seeing the net full of fish, remembered that this has happened once before. "It's the Lord!" he gasps.

The next sound they heard was a splash, as impetuous Peter dove in and swam to shore. There is something in me that is glad he responded that way. We might think he'd swim in the other direction since he had denied even knowing Jesus only a month or so earlier. But Peter, unlike Judas, seems to have known that forgiveness was waiting for him there on the shore.

Three times Peter denied even knowing Jesus. It was a cowardly thing to do, more despicable in some ways even than Judas' calculated betrayal. Peter was always the first to speak up, to pledge his allegiance to Jesus again and again. Surely his betrayal must have deeply affected the morale of all the disciples.

The disciples brought the boat to shore, filled with fish.

On the shore was a fire, with fish cooking. Jesus had prepared breakfast for His disciples. Even though He was the risen Lord, even after all He had been through, He was ever the servant Lord, caring even for their basic needs. He is, as always, the example. "Come and have breakfast," Jesus says.

As the disciples gathered around Jesus, there was a feeling of uncertainty. They didn't immediately recognize who it was. "And none of the disciples dared ask, 'Who are you?' They knew it was the Lord."

After breakfast, Jesus gave Peter three chances to reaffirm the love that he had denied three times. As always, it is a question Jesus used. "Do you love me?" To Peter's nervous answers Jesus responded "Feed my sheep."

Jesus uttered not one word of condemnation for Peter's betrayals, only affirmation of the calling he had received three years earlier. Though Peter forgot that he was supposed to be a "fisher of men" and went back to fishing for fish, Jesus says nothing about it. No condemnation, only love, affirmation, and a hot breakfast for a weary fisherman who had come a long way, but had a longer way to go still.

EL SHADDAI

El Shaddai, El Shaddai, El Elyon na Adonai,
Age to age You're still the same,
By the power of the name.
El Shaddai, El Shaddai, Erekamka na Adonai,
We will praise and lift You high
El Shaddai.

Through Your love and through the ram,
You saved the son of Abraham.
And by the power of Your hand,
Turned the sea into dry land.
To the outcast on her knees
You were the God who really sees.
And by Your might You set Your children free.

El Shaddai, El Shaddai, El Elyon na Adonai,
Age to age You're still the same,
By the power of the name.
El Shaddai, El Shaddai, Erekamka na Adonai,
We will praise and lift You high
El Shaddai.

Through the years You made it clear
That the time of Christ was near.
Though the people failed to see
What Messiah ought to be.
Though Your Word contained the plan,
They just could not understand,
Your most awesome work was done
Through the frailty of Your Son.

El Shaddai, El Shaddai, El Elyon na Adonai,
Age to age You're still the same,
By the power of the name.

El Shaddai, El Shaddai, Erekamka na Adonai,
We will praise and lift You high
El Shaddai.

Though God is One[1] He is known in the Old Testament by many names, which reveal different aspects of His nature:

- He is powerful.
- He is above all others.
- He is all-seeing.

I suppose the possibilities are infinite even as He is Infinite. This song attempts to present the paradox of Jesus by focusing on a few of these names. First let me "unpack" the Hebrew.

El means, "God." The particle appears a lot, especially in Hebrew names. My name is "Micha-el." In Hebrew it is a rhetorical question and is translated, "Who is like God?" (The answer is, of course, no one is like God.) "Dani-el" means, "God is my judge." "Jo-el" means, "Yahweh is God." Usually a name that contains the particle *el* tells us something about God.

Shaddai means "strong" or "mighty." The picture is that of a strong arm. From time to time in the Old Testament God threatens to "uncover His arm." That means the enemies of Israel had better get lost!

God first revealed Himself as El Shaddai to Abram when He confirmed the covenant of circumcision with him.[2] It was then that He promised Abram that he would be the father of many nations and changed his name accordingly from Abram, which means "exalted father," to Abraham,

which means "father of many." The next time He appeared to Abraham God demonstrated His power by obliterating Sodom and Gomorrah.[3]

El Elyon means "God Most High," or the God who is above all the other gods. During Christmas we sing "in Excelsus Deo." That is the Latin rendering of *El Elyon*. The Lord also revealed this name first to Abram. Abram had just rescued Lot from captivity to an alliance of pagan kings. On his way back home he encounters a mysterious priest named Melchizedek, a priest of "God Most High." Melchizedek imparts a barocha, or blessing, on Abram in the name of El Elyon. By that special name God was revealing to Abram that He was above all the pagan gods. He had just demonstrated His supremacy by granting Abram the power to defeat the powerful alliance in battle. Abram, in turn, gives Melchizedek a tithe of the spoils he had won in battle.

Na Adonai simply means, "Oh, Lord." *Na* is called the particle of entreaty. We see it both in the words *hosanna* ("Oh, save!") and *maranatha* ("Oh, Lord, come!"). *Adonai* is the common word for "lord." *Erekamka na Adonai* is a phrase from Psalm 18:1, which means, "I love you, oh, Lord!"

The translated version of the chorus looks like this:

> Almighty God, Almighty God,
> God Most High, Oh, Lord!
> Age to age You're still the same
> By the power of the Name.
> Almighty God, Almighty God,
> I will love You, Oh, Lord!
> We will praise and lift You high,
> Almighty God!

Through His various names and acts of power, the Lord revealed Himself to the people of the Old Testament, and

by those names He still reveals Himself to us today. He spared Isaac by providing a ram at the last minute.[4] He parted the sea so the Israelites could cross over on dry land.[5] To the outcast, Hagar, about to die of thirst in the desert, He showed a spring of water thereby revealing Himself as the "the Living One who sees me."[6]

Though He is revealed as the loving Creator and Father in the Old Testament, by and large, His power and might are the focus.

Yet when Jesus, the Son of God, appears, power is not the focus even though He does display His power over the winds and waves, over the devil and his demons. Jesus' ministry is characterized by weakness. The disciples are hardly a dazzling bunch of "movers and shakers." In the end Jesus is rejected and crucified "in weakness." How could El Shaddai be the Father of such a Son? Jesus strikes no one dead for confronting Him. He becomes tired and hungry. The ultimate paradox is that he dies. The miracle of the cross, says Buechner, is that there was no miracle!

Though God had spoken the universe into existence and displayed His power to the children of Israel, the most awesome accomplishment of El Shaddai was made possible only through the frailty of His only Son. Jesus died for you and me. By God's power He rose again, but we must never forget that first He died.

GOD'S OWN FOOL

It seems I've imagined Him all of my life,
As the wisest of all of mankind.
But if God's holy wisdom is foolish to men,
He must have seemed out of His mind.
For even His family said He was mad.
And the priests said a demon's to blame.
For God in the form of this angry young man
Could not have seemed perfectly sane.

When we in our foolishness thought we were wise,
He played the fool and He opened our eyes.
When we in our weakness believed we were strong,
He became helpless to show we were wrong.
And so we follow God's own fool,
For only the foolish can tell.
Believe the unbelievable,
And come be a fool as well.

So come lose your life for a carpenter's son,
For a madman who died for a dream.
Then you'll have the faith His first followers had,
And you'll feel the weight of the beam.
So surrender the hunger to say you must know.
Have the courage to say "I believe!"
For the power of paradox opens your eyes
And blinds those who say they can see.

When we in our foolishness thought we were wise,
He played the fool and He opened our eyes.
When we in our weakness believed we were strong,
He became helpless to show we were wrong.
And so we follow God's own fool,
For only the foolish can tell.

Believe the unbelievable,
And come be a fool as well.

In 1989 I did a radio special for the Moody Broadcast Network called, "The Life," which included songs from the trilogy of the same name as well as some commentary on the major themes in the life of Christ. Listeners were able, through a 1-800 number, to call in and interact with the program. We received a few thousand calls, almost all of which were encouraging. Even some people who differed somewhat from my interpretations voiced their differences graciously and in an encouraging way. I welcomed those kinds of responses.

Out of all of the calls, four were from irate people. Some of them attacked the network, saying that they were surprised that Moody would associate itself with someone like me! (I must confess, I wondered about that myself!) Some were angry about the style of the music, saying that it was too loud and drowned out the words. (I wondered if simply turning down their radios would have solved that problem.) The response I remember most painfully was from a man who said, "You are satanic!"

I honestly could relate to the other complaints. But satanic?

This man was upset about the song, "God's Own Fool," which is a metaphorical piece that connects the foolishness of the gospel to Jesus. Others have been upset by the song too. One church sent a formal judgment saying I was forbidden to ever sing in it again. A lady called the record company to complain, and I called her back to see if I could explain. I discovered that she had only heard a part

of the chorus in the car and hadn't even listened to the verses.

No amount of explaining on my part has ever been able to satisfy any of these people. My own pastor, as well as the ministry board that oversees what I do, said the song is indeed biblical and allows me to sing it. The following words are for those who really want to hear what I am trying to say. I'll try to be clear without getting defensive, although it's rather like explaining a joke. Explaining it kind of takes the punch away.

The song is based on 1 Corinthians 1:25: "For the foolishness of God is wiser than man's wisdom, and the weakness of God is stronger than man's strength."

Paul was writing to a group of believers who were experiencing the gifts of the Spirit in a remarkable way, even though they were, at the same time, immature and divisive. Immorality had been a problem in the church almost from the beginning. Paul had already written an earlier letter

about that particular problem, which had been either mis-understood or ignored. The Corinthians were abusing the Lord's Table and disregarding the poor. All in all they sound like a typical American Christian church!

In the introduction to the letter, Paul wants to talk about Jesus as the wisdom and power of God. In light of the Corinthian situation, he chooses to contrast the wisdom of God with the foolishness of men. By comparison, he says, the gospel is foolishness. Likewise, to reveal the impo-tence of worldly power, Paul says, God chose the "weak things of this world to shame the strong." "Jesus," he says elsewhere, "was crucified in weakness."[1]

Looking at the gospel straight on, without comfortably wrapping it in our culture, it is foolish. An itinerant Gali-lean carpenter says He is God. A virgin birth. A resurrec-tion after three days. Apart from the Spirit's enabling us to have faith in the wisdom of it (for it is, after all, Wisdom) these things are impossible to believe.

I tend to be highly suspicious of people who try to make these impossible concepts make sense. There is surely a place for intellect in the kingdom, or else God wouldn't have given us brains. Some of the greatest minds in the history of the world have embraced the gospel, but like Pascal, they were always ready to confess the inadequacy of the human mind to grasp the wisdom of God and there-fore the absolute necessity for faith. That is not anti-intellectualism but rather humility. Through the Incarnation, Truth became a person. All the wisdom of God is found in Jesus.

The focus of the gospel is Jesus, of course. And if it is foolishness to the world, then He is seen to be the fool. The Gospels bear abundant witness to that conclusion. Why, even His own mother and brothers thought at one point that Jesus was mad![2] In the same passage where Paul talks about the foolishness of the gospel he introduces the con-

cept of the *scandalon,* or stumbling block, another metaphor for Jesus. (The metaphor of the scandalon is only applied to one other concept in the New Testament: sin! I wonder if anyone was upset with Paul for using that scandalous metaphor!)

So am I really calling Jesus a fool? Of course not! He is the Wisdom of God. But that is, after all, foolishness to men. Even as Paul played the fool with the so-called super apostles,[3] so we are called to follow One who played the fool for our sake.

MARANATHA

Maranatha *is a cry of the heart*
That's hopeful yet weary of waiting,
While it may be joyful with the burdens it bears,
It's sick with anticipating.

To long for the promised One day after day,
And the promise that soon He'd return.
It's certain that waiting's the most bitter lesson
A believing heart has to learn.

Maranatha. *How desperate we are just to see Your face!*
Maranatha. *To finally fall in Your strong embrace!*
A trumpet, a call, and that will be all,
Though it's not yet the hour, the minutes are ticking away.

Maranatha *is the shout of the few,*
Who for so long in history've been hiding,
Who truly believe that the sound of that call,
Might actually hasten His coming.

For no eye has seen and no ear has yet heard
And no mind has ever conceived
The joy of the moment when He will appear,
To the wonder of all who believe.

Maranatha. *How desperate we are just to see Your face!*
Maranatha. *To finally fall in Your strong embrace!*
A trumpet, a call, and that will be all,
Though it's not yet the hour, the minutes are ticking away.

One of my favorite authors, Brennan Manning, tells a story of a young boy who became obsessed with the image of a face that appeared in the natural rock formations on the side of a mountain. If you stood just in the right place, you could see the outline of the forehead, nose, and chin of what appeared to be the face of a kindly man. Every day the boy would go up into the hills and stare for hours at the face. Soon he reached the conclusion that this was the image of someone who would someday come to his town, and that he might actually get the opportunity to meet the gentle and mysterious person behind the face.

The boy began hanging around the docks, examining the face of each person who would get off a boat, looking for that one special face. As years went by the boy became a man, but he stubbornly kept studying the face on the mountain and going to the docks every day to see if he could find "that face."

One day, years later, when he was very old, he asked one of the passengers who had just gotten off a ship, "Are you the face on the mountain? Is it you?"

The traveler stopped and looked at the old man for a long time. Finally he answered, "No, it's you."

The old man had gazed so intently at the face on the mountain that he had taken on its image.

All of my life I have had a deep yearning to simply see the face of Jesus, to know what He looks like. Like the boy in the story, I have resorted to seeking out His image on the faces of His children. From time to time I catch the glimpse of a smile that must be like His or I see someone express compassion as He would. To this day when someone boasts of having a vision of Him, inwardly I burn with jealousy. I wonder sometimes why seeing Him hasn't resulted in a more profound change in the person's life. Then I stop and realize that I would probably be no different. I trust that

He knows what He is doing, hiding Himself from me among His children. Still I hope that, like the old man, someday someone will see something of His face in mine.

That yearning to see Jesus is spelled out in the heart-cry, "Maranatha!" It's an Aramaic word that means "Oh Lord, come!" The exclamation comes from the particle *na*, which means "Oh" or "Please." The early Christians actually believed that the word, *maranatha*, would hasten the Lord's return.

Jesus didn't have too much to say about his Second Coming. There is really only one incident, recorded both in Matthew 24 and Mark 13. Jesus has just been raging against the hypocrisy of the Pharisees. The section in Matthew is usually referred to as the "Seven Woes," a passage that cannot be read in a "Sunday school" voice. Jesus repeats Himself in His anger, "You hypocrites, you hypocrites!" There isn't another passage like this in the New Testament.

As Jesus is leaving the temple area with His disciples, still fuming, the disciples try to distract Him by making small talk. This seems to irritate Him even more.

"Look Teacher! What massive stones!"

They are referring to the foundation stones of the temple, the largest of which were twenty to forty feet long and over six feet thick. But Jesus had been around the temple all His life. He knew what the foundation looked like. They could not distract Him.

Still seething he responds, "See those stones, not one of them will be left standing on the other. They will all be pulled down."

He is referring to the destruction of the temple in A.D. 70 by Titus. That pronouncement apparently shut the disciples up for the rest of the afternoon.

Later on, however, the disciples return to Jesus and ask Him two questions about His earlier statement: "When will

this happen?" and "What will be the sign of Your coming?" They thought that Jesus' prediction of the destruction of the temple was part of the end of the world and the Second Coming.

Jesus gives them two separate answers.

The first section of His discourse, which makes up the answer to the first question, "When will these things (the destruction of the temple) happen?" is full of concrete language. Jesus warns the disciples not to be deceived during this time, when many will claim to be the Christ. Jesus talks about wars and earthquakes. He mentions that they will sooner or later be arrested for claiming to be His disciples but that the Holy Spirit will give them words to speak when that time comes. When the actual overtaking of the temple occurs, the "abomination that causes desolation," Jesus tells His disciples to make a run for it. He has been describing an event that you can run away from, the occupation of Jerusalem by Roman soldiers, who set up their idols in the temple and finally burned the temple to the ground. Afterward the soldiers pried all the stones apart to retrieve the gold that had melted between the stones. Jesus' prophecy was perfectly fulfilled. Not one stone was left standing on another.

Then there is a radical break in Jesus' language, as He begins to answer their second question, the question of what will be the sign of the Second Coming. His language turns apocalyptic. He talks about the stars falling from the sky and the moon turning to blood. He says that two men will be in the field working, and two women grinding grain together, one will be taken, the other left. This is an event that you definitely cannot run away from!

Jesus' teaching is almost frustratingly simple. There are three or four basic points. His words have been so mixed up and sensationalized by those who, in trying to explain

what Jesus left unsaid, have made charts and graphs and hopelessly confused words that are really quite simple and profoundly comforting. These are the basic points:

1. The gospel must first be preached to all nations.[1] Jesus leaves us with a task, not with a coded message only for the "wise." This is the most concrete thing He points to.

2. When He returns everyone will know it. It will not be some secret for the elite who have figured out the puzzle. It will be like lightning flashing across the sky. "As the lightning comes from the east and flashes to the west, so will be the Coming of the Son of Man."[2]

3. No one knows the hour, not even Jesus Himself. That is hard for us to understand when we consider Jesus' oneness with the Father whom He says knows when the time will be. But let's not start trying to make up explanations for what cannot be understood.[3]

4. Because no one knows the time, His second coming will be totally unexpected. Jesus uses the story of Noah to illustrate the point that no one expected the flood (since it had never rained before then). They were eating and drinking and so on, never expecting what was coming to them. That is how Jesus' second coming will be.[4]

5. Jesus' final command is to "Watch!"[5]

Jesus leaves us, not with secret signs that only the spiritual giants can discern. No, He leaves simple and easy-to-understand instructions to His beloved children. What we're left with is not concrete pronouncements about events. ("Wars and rumors of wars" means that it's not the time yet!) He gives us words of simplicity that force us to rely on Him. We must preach the gospel to all nations, not analyze the numerical value of Gorbachev. We can take comfort that He Himself will let us know when He has returned, for we shall all see Him and absolutely no one knows the hour. Jesus leaves us with a future hope that, by

faith, transforms our present reality with Him. So what we are left with is faith, hope, and a special word that might very well hasten His coming after all, Maranatha! Oh Lord, come!

JOY IN THE JOURNEY

There is a joy in the journey.
There's a light we can love on the way.
There is a wonder and wildness to life,
And freedom for those who obey.

And all those who seek it
Shall find it. *
A pardon for all who believe.
A hope for the hopeless,
And sight for the blind. *

To all who've been born of the Spirit,
And who share incarnation with Him,
Who belong to eternity,
Stranded in time,
And weary of struggling with sin.

Forget not the hope
That's before you.
And never stop counting the cost.
Remember the hopelessness
When you were lost?

There is a joy in the journey.
There's a light we can love on the way.
There is a wonder and wildness to life,
And freedom for those who obey.

---

*Proverbs 8:17; Isaiah 42:7.

Today is Easter Sunday. I'm in a Holiday Inn in Stubenville, Ohio. Tomorrow there will be a concert here at Franciscan University, a reunion with students I have come to love and appreciate and a chance to spend some time with the monks whose devotional life and gentle simplicity I so deeply admire. But for today it's peanut butter and jelly for breakfast, a sterile room, and the wasteland of HBO. It's a joyless, ordinary, homesick day, only more so.

That first Easter was an ordinary day. A good number of the Jews were probably in the Holiday Inn halfway between their hometowns and Jerusalem, returning to the ordinariness of their daily routines, wondering to themselves how the joy of Passover could have disappeared so quickly from their hearts, thinking back to the wonderful feast of Passover as they sat in the motel, eating their peanut butter sandwiches. Jesus chose an ordinary day to transform the world and give us the chance to know joy.

Joy is hard to find on ordinary days, in the routine of daily life. If real joy is to be found it must come from the outside. On those mystical occasions when joy comes to us from beyond, the ordinary is transformed into a vehicle for true joy. The entire world can be transformed in a moment. A trip to the grocery can quickly change into an adventure. Changing a dirty diaper can become a meaningful demonstration of divine love. A hotel room in Stubenville can be transformed in an instant into a holy place where you might even be confronted with the risen Lord.

Jesus saves us not only from our sin and ourselves. He also saves us from our ordinariness. He transforms the drudgery of daily existence into a wonderful journey with Him. We see with new eyes, hear with new ears. An ordinary voice can become sweet. A simple flower is seen to possess the mystery of life. We find meaning where there was no meaning before, precisely because Jesus brings new

meaning to everything, even the most meaningless of days. We find joy where before there was only dullness of heart because, beyond ourselves, Jesus has come, the true bringer of joy.

C. S. Lewis was drawn to Christ through an experience he described as being "surprised by joy." Lewis's first experience of joy came via the ordinary. His brother, Warren, had fashioned a toy garden from the top of a biscuit tin.

> Once in those very early days, my brother brought into the nursery the lid of a biscuit tin which he had covered with moss and garnished with twigs and flowers so as to make it a toy garden or a toy forest. That was the first beauty I ever knew. . . . As long as I live, my imagination of Paradise will retain something of my brother's toy garden.[1]

The Lord used that ordinary piece of tin to create an experience so powerful that it shaped the mind of Christianity's greatest contemporary writer. Having briefly tasted it as a boy, his life became preoccupied with finding that source of joy for which his heart ached. He finally found it, almost a lifetime later, in the love of Christ. Lewis's hunger for joy was not satisfied until he found love, for joy is simply another word for love.

In one of Jesus' final words to His disciples and to us He spoke of love and joy:

> "As the Father has loved me, so have I loved you. Now remain in my love. If you obey my commands, you will remain in my love, just as I have obeyed my Father's commands and remain in His love. I have told you this so that my joy may be in you and that your joy may be complete. My command is this: Love each other as I have loved you"[2]

In those four simple verses Jesus gives us the secret to both love and complete joy: obedience. The three concepts turn around each other like planets circling one bright sun. In words that can almost be spoken in a single breath, Jesus gives to Lewis and to you and to me all that our hearts could hunger for.

There is a joy in this journey. It comes from obedience. It comes from beyond. It comes in spite of the ordinary, or perhaps because of it. It is another word for love, which is another word for Jesus.

JESUS, LET US
COME TO KNOW YOU

*Jesus, let us
Come to know You.
Let us see You.
Face to face.
Touch us, hold us,
Use us, mold us,
Only let us
Live in You.*

*Jesus, draw us
Ever nearer,
Hold us in Your
Loving arms.
Wrap us in Your
Gentle presence.
And when the end comes
Bring us home.*

NOTES

THE INCARNATION

The Final Word
1. 1 Cor. 4:20.
2. 1 Cor. 1:24.

The Promise
1. Gen. 3:15.

To the Mystery
1. Isa. 55:8.

Carmen Christi
1. Pliny, Letters to Trajan. Letter 10, sec. 97.
2. Suetonius, Life of the Deified Claudius, 25.4.
3. Phil. 2:6–8, emphases added.
4. Phil. 2:9–11.
5. Luke 14:11.
6. Matt. 20:26, NKJV.

Now That I've Held Him in My Arms
1. Gen. 3:15.

Spirit of the Age
1. Jer. 31:15.
2. 2 Thess. 1:10.

THE MINISTRY

The Voice of the Child
1. Luke 2:47.
2. Luke 2:48.

The Baptism
1. John 3:5.
2. Mark 1:4.
3. Matt. 26:39.

Scandalon
1. Isa. 8:14.
2. Isa. 53:3.
3. Mark 6:3.
4. Matt. 15:12.
5. Mark 2:3–7.
6. John 6:60.
7. Luke 1:44.
8. John 1:29, NKJV.

The Lamb Is a Lion
1. John 2:17.

The Nazarene
1. Phil. 2:6.
2. 1 John 3:2.

The Wedding
1. Acts 2:47.
2. Acts 2:13.
3. Isa. 25:6.

What Will It Take
1. Matt. 19:16ff.
2. Matt. 19:22.
3. Mark 2:1–12.
4. Matt. 9:1.

Loneliness
1. Mark 3:33.
2. John 6:15.
3. Matt. 14:13.
4. Luke 5:16.

The Things We Leave Behind
1. See Luke 18:28ff.
2. Mark 10:50.
3. John 4:28–29.
4. Matt. 9:20ff.
5. Luke 7:11ff.
6. Mark 14:3.
7. John 11.
8. John 8:36.

Distressing Disguise
1. Luke 9:58.
2. Matt. 17:24ff.
3. Luke 18:28.

The Stranger
1. John 1:10–11.
2. Matt. 25:35.
3. Rom. 8:22.
4. Mark 4:41.

Nathaniel
1. John 1:49.
2. Gen. 28.

THE PASSION

Ride On to Die
1. Mark 10:46ff.
2. John 12:17.
3. John 11:35.

Come to the Table
1. John 12:47.

Traitor's Look
1. Matt. 26:15.
2. Matt. 10:4.

Crown Him!
1. 1 Sam. 8:7.
2. Zech. 12:10.
3. Isa. 53:5.
4. Rev. 19:11–13.

Known by the Scars
1. Zech. 13:6.
2. Rev. 5:1–5, NKJV.
3. Gal. 6:17; see also, 2 Cor. 1:5; 1 Pet. 4:13.

Here I Stand
1. Hab. 1:13.

This Must Be the Lamb
1. John 1:29, NKJV.
2. John 6:27.
3. Exod. 12.
4. 1 Cor. 5:7.
5. Exod. 12:46; Num. 9:12.

Love Crucified Arose
1. Col. 1:18.

He Was Heard
1. Heb. 4:14–5:10.
2. Heb. 9:28.

El Shaddai
1. Deut. 6:4.
2. Gen. 17.
3. Gen. 19.
4. Gen. 22.
5. Exod. 14:15ff.
6. Gen. 16:9ff.

God's Own Fool
1. 2 Cor. 13:4.
2. Mark 3:21.
3. 2 Cor. 11:13.

Maranatha
1. Mark 13:10.
2. Matt. 24:27.
3. Matt. 24:36.
4. Matt. 24:37ff.
5. Mark 13:37.

Joy in the Journey
1. C. S. Lewis, *Surprised by Joy* (NY: Harcourt, Brace, Jovanovich, 1966), 7.
2. John 15:9–12.

Michael Card publishes a bi-annual ministry news and editorial publication called "The Life." For this free publication write to:

> Creative Trust
> ATTN: "The Life" Newsletter
> P.O. Box 871
> Franklin, TN 37605

DISCOGRAPHY

1990	*The Way of Wisdom* (The Ancient Faith, Vol. II)	SP1223	Sparrow Records
1989	*The Beginning* (The Ancient Faith, Vol. I)	SP1219	Sparrow Records
1989	*Sleep Sound in Jesus*	SP1179	Sparrow Records
1988	*Present Reality*	SP1155	Sparrow Records
1987	*The Final Word* (The Life, Vol. III)	SP1126	Sparrow Records
1985	*Scandalon* (The Life, Vol. II)	SP1117	Sparrow Records
1983	*Known By the Scars* (The Life, Vol. I)	SP1097	Sparrow Records
1983	*Legacy*	CD02457	Benson
1981	*First Light*	CD02457	Benson